Princess Na
(Volum

Ouida

Alpha Editions

This edition published in 2024

ISBN 9789362092946

Design and Setting By
Alpha Editions
www.alphaedis.com
Email - info@alphaedis.com

Contents

CHAPTER XXXIV.

When Yseulte had recovered enough to travel, he took her to the Italian lakes for awhile, to restore her to her usual health and strength, and distract her thoughts from what had befallen her at Amyôt. With the beginning of winter they returned, and made their home for awhile in the great hotel of the Boulevard St. Germain, which he hated, and where he intended to remain for the briefest time that could suffice for the fulfilment of those social duties of which Friederich Othmar never ceased to remind him. There his mother's apartments had been prepared for his wife, and every grace and attraction that the art and the taste of the day could add to them had been added, as though the most solicitous affection had presided over the preparation of them. All the preferences she had shown in the country had been remembered and gratified; whatever she had liked best in colour, in treatment, in art, in flowers, in marble, had been consulted or reproduced in Paris; and even a large dog to which she had taken a fancy at Amyôt had been brought thence from the kennels, and was lying before the fire when she entered.

A much older and far wiser woman would have been persuaded to believe, as she believed, that in all this delicate *prévenance* for her pleasures and her preferences the tenderest love had spoken. She could not divine the self-reproach of her husband's conscience, which made him sensible that he perforce denied her so much that was her due, and made him proportionately eager to atone for that denial by every material enjoyment and outward mark of affection and of homage. All those who surrounded him, all his acquaintances, his household, and his dependents, imagined that he loved his young wife. The person who was in nowise deceived was Friederich Othmar.

'He is like a Sultan,' thought the old man angrily, 'a Sultan who loads the women of his zenana with ropes of pearls and emeralds as big as pigeon's eggs, that they may not perceive that he only visits them twice a year!'

By the law of the attraction of contrasts, there had arisen a mutual attachment between her and Baron Fritz: the unscrupulous old man, for whom as for Turcaret the whole world was composed of shareholders, felt more reverence and tenderness for Yseulte than he ever felt in his life for anyone; and she, who only saw his devotion to Othmar, his admirable manners, his shrewd wit, and his paternal kindness to herself, grew fond of, and grateful to, him, and was wholly ignorant of that mercilessness and selfishness which would have immolated all mankind to the service of his personal ambitions, and to which all morality or humanity appeared as absurd as they did to Fouquet or to Talleyrand.

Friederich Othmar incessantly strove to inspire her with his own passion for the House he adored, and though he failed because she was too thoroughly patrician in all her instincts to easily welcome such impressions, and was more apt to share her husband's disdain for all such ambitions, he did succeed in persuading her that the future content of Othmar himself would depend on the measure of the interest which he would take in those great fortunes of which he held the key.

'Understand this, my child,' he would say, 'a man in old age never forgives himself for the occasions which he has let slip in youth; and every man who in youth is *désœuvré*, pays for it heavily when age has come. Otho is a clever man, but he has the sickness of his century; he is indifferent to everything' ('even to you!' he thought impatiently). 'We call it the malady of the time; I do not know that we are right. It existed in Petronius Arbiter's, but it had no existence in our immediate forefathers'. However, you do not care for abstract discussions; you care for Otho. Well, let us confine ourselves to Otho. Nowadays, he is still a young man; he thinks he can afford to despise all things because he has strength, and health, and every form of enjoyment accessible to him—and he is certainly rich enough to play at cynicism all day if it amuse him most.'

'He is no cynic,' said Yseulte, quickly.

Baron Fritz smiled.

'A little of Alceste, surely? You read "Le Misanthrope," even at your convent, I imagine? My dear child, people always desire the fate they have not. Alfred de Vigny, with his sixteen quarterings, was always in rebellion against the fate of the poor gentleman; Otho, one of the richest men in Europe, is always rebelling against his riches as a chain and a species of dishonour. Now, it is for you to reconcile him to them; it is for you to persuade him that in the interests of his House lie those occupations and obligations which will not pall upon him as he grows older. I have known men weary of love and pleasure, but I have never known them weary of ambition. Otho scorns vulgar ambitions, but there are those which are not vulgar. In finance, as in life, there is no standing still. In his present mood he would be delighted if ruin were possible to us; it is not possible. Short of a European war that should last thirty years, nothing can harm us much. Still, no great house can long stand without a chief who cares for its welfare and honour. Like Catherine II., "je lis l'avenir dans le passé." A wise statesman has always the past of the world spread out before him like an ordnance map for his guidance. So may we also, in the past history of such houses as our own, see what has led to their ruin, and so guide ourselves to avoid those evils in our own case. Now, nothing has been so commonly the cause of *krach* in financial establishments as their being afflicted with imprudent or indifferent members. Otho is not very often imprudent, but he is entirely indifferent. Certainly,' continued the Baron, with pardonable pride, 'the Maison d'Othmar is too solidly established, too greatly important to the public life of Europe, to be easily imperilled by a young man's foibles. Still, I cannot disguise from myself the fact that when I am no more there will be no check on his eccentricities, no stimulus to his apathy. He will be ill served because he will at once expect too much virtue from men, and observe them with too little suspicion. The ship is sound and safe, and sure to have fair winds, but if the man at her helm be reading his Horace or his La Bruyère instead of steering by his chart, the ship may founder in clear weather and calm seas. You understand me?'

Metaphor was very unusual to him; he only condescended to use it for sake of making his meaning clearer to the feebleness of a feminine mind.

'Yes, I understand quite well,' she replied, with a little sigh. 'But I have no influence; he would think me impertinent; and I am sure no one will care for the honour of the House more truly than he.'

'Commercially speaking, there are two kinds of honour,' said Friederich Othmar. 'The fantastic and visionary one he will always maintain, but the practical one, which lies in doing your utmost for all the interests centred in yours, he will neglect. If I were to tell him that we must collapse to-morrow, he would give up everything, down to his pet edition of Marcus Aurelius, to satisfy our debts; but if I were to tell him also how many financial schemes and companies would fall with us, he would only reply that the world would be exceedingly well rid of so many scoundrels. The honour is safe with him, doubtless, but the welfare is not. I shall not live for ever; I shall probably only live a very few years more. You must persuade your husband that his true duties and pleasures will lie in those ambitions which his fathers have bequeathed to him. I know that he and you would like to extinguish the House of Othmar financially, and dwell at Amyôt with no remembrance of the world. That is a lover's dream. My dear, simplicity and solitude are impossible in our society; a shepherd's peace is not attainable by a man whom the world claims. If I were to die to-morrow, and Otho to remain as indifferent to his own interests as he is now, all that I have done, all that his predecessors have done, would crumble away in ten or twenty years like so much soft sandstone in a succession of wet winters. He would not resent it now, but when he should be fifty years old he would resent it bitterly; he would never pardon himself. It is from this possibility that your influence must protect him.'

She hesitated, with a blush upon her face.

'I have no influence,' she said timidly. 'He knows so much better, so much more than I——'

'Obtain influence over him,' said the old man curtly; 'for if you do not, someone else will. Nay, my dear, pardon me; do not be hurt by my plain speaking. Such men as Otho are always influenced by women; he should be so now by you; he will be so if you will leave off worshipping him timidly, making him your law and your religion, and realise that you are an exquisitely lovely woman, with mind enough not to be the mere toy of any man. You are very young, it is true, but you have grown ten years in a few months. You must remember that to be in love is very agreeable, no doubt, but you are not his mistress; you are his wife. You must not think only of the immediate moment, but of the far future when he will not be in love with you, *ma belle*, nor you with him, but when you may still influence him nobly and wisely, and he may find in you his safest friend.'

Yseulte listened, with a little sigh.

It seemed to her as if all her happy illusions were taking wing, like the group of amorini which flew away from a weeping nymph on the ceiling of her room, which had been painted by Bourgereau. They were seated in one of her own apartments, a very bower of primroses and white lilac, panelled in the Louis Seize style, with Bourgereau's charming children in groups within each panel above the satin couches. Between the curtains, there were glimpses through the windows of the cedars and wellingtonias of the gardens. Without, it was a chilly winter's day, but within, it was warm as summer, mellow with soft colour, fragrant with innumerable flowers; even to this great hotel of the Boulevard S. Germain, which had always seemed to Othmar the most oppressive and detestable of all his many mansions, the advent of Yseulte had brought a grace and light and sweetness as of young and innocent life, a charm of home to these splendid and desolate suites of rooms. Her dogs lay on the hearth, her voice called the peacocks in the lonely gardens, her scores of Beethoven and Schubert and Berlioz lay open on the grand pianos. Even the look of the great bouquets in the Japanese bowls and the jars of Saxe and Sèvres was different: her hand had added a rose there, a fern here; they were flowers which were there because she loved them, not only because they served for decorations grouped by skilful servants as mere masses of colour. The great house, sombre in its Bourbon stateliness, magnificent in its architecture, but oppressive in its too continual display of wealth, was no longer 'une maison sans musique, une ruche sans abeilles;' it had gained a charm which was none the less perceptible because undefinable and impalpable, as the scent of the tea-roses in the tall Sèvres jars. But Friederich Othmar was more sensible of this than was the possessor of the house and of her. Friederich Othmar, who had lived for fifty years and more without perceiving that he had never had, or wished to have, a home, perceived that his nephew had one and scarcely appreciated it. Friederich Othmar himself became suddenly alive to the pleasure of finding something home-like in that corner of her boudoir where she drew a Japanese screen between him and the draught from the windows, brought him his cup of green tea, and listened with an interest fresh and unfeigned to his anecdotes, his reminiscences, and his counsels: but he found Othmar there less often than he would have wished.

'He will be glad of that *coin du feu* some day,' he thought angrily; annoyed by a neglect which Yseulte herself did not perceive. She had been used to solitude; she was neither vain nor exacting; she understood that everything could not be in Paris altogether as it had been at Amyôt; and if she gave a sigh to that necessity, she bravely and tranquilly accepted it. The great world was about her with its demands, its solicitations, its tyrannies over time and thought; she had little leisure for meditation; the Countess Othmar could not escape the social obligations of her position or avoid its ceremonies and its courtesies.

She remained much graver and simpler than her contemporaries were; she cared for none of the noisy amusements of modern fashion; the world of pleasure seemed to her, on the whole, a little vulgar, a little tiresome, astonishingly monotonous, even in its feverish search for the untried and the startling. But at the same time she could not escape from its demands, and their effects upon her, and the counsels of Friederich Othmar incessantly reminded her that she could best serve the honour of the name she bore by making Europe admire and praise her. It was a counsel which contained the seeds of danger; but he read her character aright.

'Voilà une qui ne *cascadera* jamais,' said the Baron to himself in his tongue of the Boulevards. He was infinitely proud of, and delighted with her; he gave her the most magnificent presents, bought her the rarest of jewels. He accompanied her constantly in her drives and to the opera, and even in the visits which she paid.

'It is Baron Fritz whom Othmar's marriage has reformed!' said a pretty woman, who had long considered the silver-haired financier as her own especial prey. He took a paternal pleasure in the admiration which the rare patrician graces of the girl awoke in that *tout Paris* which he had long considered the lawgiver of the universe.

'If you had been Marie Antoinette, there might have been no revolution,' he said jestingly to her. 'You would never have flirted with Ferson, nor would you have played at shepherdessing, or worn a mask in the Palais Royal.'

'I think I should only have thought of France,' she answered.

'Which would not have prevented you from going to the guillotine, I dare say,' said the Baron. 'Nations are the concentrated distillation of the ingratitude of men. There is only one thing which one can always count on with absolute certainty, and that is, the general and individual thanklessness.'

Nothing was further from his thoughts than to cloud over the trust, confidence, and faith of her innocent optimism. He spoke as he thought and felt, and as a long experience of mankind had taught him to do, without reflecting that he dropped the bitterness of gall into a fair and limpid spring, which had seen nothing above its waters save the white lily-cups and the blue heavens.

'She will be robbed right and left endlessly if she be not taught a little mistrust,' he said to Othmar himself, who replied:

'Let her be robbed of everything rather than of her illusions. This is the only loss from which we never recover.'

'What an absurd idea!' thought the Baron, who had never cherished any illusions at all, and had found life exceedingly entertaining and enjoyable without them.

The practical mind can no more understand the regrets of the meditative one than a manufacturer, spending his days by choice amidst the roar of steam wheels and the ledgers of a counting-house, can understand the artist's anguish when he is shut up in a city garret whence he cannot see a sunset or a sunrise.

'The woes of the body, I grant, may be too much for one's philosophy,' the Baron was wont to say. 'With the gout, or neuralgia, or sciatica, Seneca's self might fail to retain serenity. But the sorrows of the emotions or of the imagination are so entirely fictitious that anyone, by the exercise of a little self-control, may put them aside completely.'

'What! Even the losses of death?' objected some one once.

The Baron smiled:

'Death cannot affect you very greatly unless you have already committed an act of unwisdom—that is, have already attached yourself to some other life than your own.'

'Then where is love?' said his interlocutor.

'Where it has always been,' said Friederich Othmar, 'chiefly in the senses partially in the imagination. When we have both the senses and the imagination under the control of our temperate judgment, it cannot disturb us seriously. In my youth, and even in my maturity,' he continued, with complacence, 'I have dallied with love as well as other men, but the moment that I felt that any one passion was likely to exercise undue influence upon me, I withdrew myself from it. To break a chain is difficult, but never to let it be forged is easy.'

He thought it his duty to put his young favourite on her guard against all the deceptions and delusions which the world prepares for its novices; he told her much more than her husband would have done of all the intricacies and meanings of the varied life which was about her, gave her the key to many of its secrets, and the hidden biographies of many of its personages.

'You are in the world, you must understand the world,' he said to her; 'if not, it will be a mere labyrinth to you, and you will be lost in it. You need not become a *mondaine* with your heart, but you must become one with your head, or the *mondaines* will devour you. It is not necessary that you should gamble or swear or get into debts for your petticoats, as they do; but it is necessary that you should understand the society of your time. At Amyôt you may be a young saint, as heaven meant you to be, but in Paris you must be able to hold your own against those who are the reverse of saints. Otho ought to teach you all this himself, but he will not, so you must listen to me. I have not been so engrossed in the gold market all my days that I do not know *la haute gomme* down to the ground. In my leisure I have always gone into the world: the boudoir of a pretty woman is always much more amusing than a card-table or a pistol-gallery. *L'Ecole des Femmes* is the one to which every wise man goes.'

He paused, with a consciousness that he had better not pursue that theme.

'My child,' he resumed, as the carriage rolled down the Bois, 'you are not seventeen; you are in love with your husband; you sweep your conscience every morning with a palm-leaf to make sure there is no little film of a cobweb left in it; you think life is such a simple and beautiful thing that you have only to get up and go to bed as the sun does. You hear quantities of compliments, but you pay no attention to them; you are altogether as innocent as a flower, and you are quite exquisite like that—it suits you; but, all the same, you cannot go on like that for ever. Men might let you, for we are not as black as we are painted, but women will not. It is from women that your sorrows will come, that your perception of evil will come, that your enemies will come. Satan, pardon me the word, would take off his hat to you and pass by on the other side, for he, too, is not as black as he has been painted. But women will not feel what Satan would feel; they are much more hard to touch. It is women whom you must try to understand; you can analyse without imbibing, as chemists do poisons.'

'Must one analyse at all?' said Yseulte, a little wistfully.

Such abrupt and familiar allusions to Satan disturbed the awe in which she had been reared at Faïel; but she was growing used to the perception that all the things which she held most sacred were mere Mother Goose's tales to the world in general, and to understand why her cousin Clothilde, who had her emblazoned chair at S. Philippe du Roule and occupied it so regularly, and was so heedful all Lent to wear the strictest mourning costume without a shred of lace, had yet not a grain of real religion in her. She began to comprehend what Blanchette had meant by all her rapturous felicitations, and sometimes the proud and austere young soul of her was humiliated to think that these mere material pleasures should have any attraction for her: she felt that her grandmother's ascetic and haughty teachings would have condemned such joys as mundane and vulgar. But the pleasure of them was there, nevertheless, and she was too honest in her self-analysis to dissimulate before her conscience. Unworldly as temperament and education alike made her, Yseulte was feminine enough and accessible enough to such vanities for all the possessions into which she entered to amuse and please her with their novelty and the sense of power which they gave. She was but a child in years, and the large households deferential to her slightest word, the grand equipages ready for her whim and fancy, the beautiful horses which bore her with the fleetness of the wind, the vast houses through which she could wander, conscious that she was the mistress of them all, the innumerable beauties of art which they contained, the caskets and coffers full of jewels and baubles, all these things beguiled her time and gratified that pride which a very young girl always feels in the sudden assumption of womanhood. She began to understand why all her companions at Faïel had thought her so fortunate. Her serious and spiritual nature made her feel a little ashamed at finding so much interest in such earthly treasures; in her self-examination she reproved herself, and almost contemned herself. But she was too young not to take such irresistible delight in all these things as a child takes in butterflies or poppies; it was delightful to say 'I wish,' and see her wishes accomplished as by magic; it was charming to give away right and left, as out of a bottomless purse; it was amusing to command, to confer, to be regarded as the source of all favours and all fortune, as the people of Amyôt and the household of Paris regarded her. In time, the delicacy of her taste, the seriousness of her intelligence, might probably make these possessions and privileges pall on her; in time she would see sycophancy where she now saw only devotion, and grow weary of a loyalty only rooted in self-interest; but, at the onset, life was to her like a fairy story, her empire was one on which the sun never set and in which the spring-time never waned.

Othmar never said one word which could have served to disenchant her. Conscious that he could not give her all the singleness of love which was her due, he strove to atone for any wrong he did her so by multiplying around her every physical gratification, and giving her an unlimited power of self-indulgence.

In this new life she was like a child who stands amidst the bewilderment of its crowd of New Year presents; sometimes she thought of herself as she had been six months before, sitting in the shadow of the stone cloisters at Faïel, in her dust-coloured convent frock, with the blue ribbon of merit crossing her breast and some holy book open on her hands, with a kind of wondering pity and strangeness, and a sense of being herself far, very far, away from any kinship with that sad grey figure.

That so little of egotism was aroused in her in this hot-house existence which she led, was due to the generosity and simplicity of her instincts, on which the contagion of worldly influences had little power. To send a silver crucifix to Faïel, or a piece of fine lace to Nicole, still gave her greater pleasure than to wear her own great diamonds or see the crowds in the Champs Elysées look after her carriage with its liveries of black velvet and white satin.

Meanwhile she had the natural feeling of every unselfish and generous nature, that her life was not full enough of thought for others. It was difficult for her at her age to know what to do, so as to carry out those theories of self-sacrifice which training and temperament alike made a religion to her.

Friederich Othmar, when he discovered this, told her, with some impatience, that the House of Othmar always did what was expected of it in this respect, and that its women had no occasion to trouble their heads with such matters.

'Wherever we have been located we have always been good citizens,' he said, with truth. 'We have always borne our due share of public expenditure or public almsgiving; perhaps more than our due share. Myself, I believe that all that sort of charity is a vast mistake. It is intended as a sop to the wolves, but you cannot feed wolves on sops. They will always want your blood, however they may lick up your mess.'

Yseulte remembered that S. Francis had proved that even wolves may be tamed into affection and usefulness; but though she believed firmly in that legend, she hesitated to put it forward, even as an allegory, as evidence against the arguments of the Baron. She did not lack courage, nor even that truest courage, the courage of opinion, but she had been reared in the old traditions of high breeding, which make contradiction a vulgarity, and, from the young to the old, an offence.

'I hope you will not make yourself into a sort of Judith Montefiore,' continued the Baron irritably. 'We are not Jews. Jews must do that kind of thing to get themselves tolerated. We could forgive them the Crucifixion, but we cannot forgive them their percentage. Though we are not Jews, Otho has already done some Quixotic things in the Montefiore fashion. I hope you will not encourage him to continue them.'

'Tell me what they were,' she said, with the light in her eyes and the colour in her face.

'Not I,' said the Baron; 'I much prefer to see him smoking à Londrès at the Jockey.'

'Had he ever any very great sorrow?' she ventured to ask.

'None, my dear, but what he chose to make for himself,' replied Friederich Othmar, with contempt. 'Do you remember Joubert's regret that he could not write his thoughts on the bark of trees by merely looking at them?— well, Otho's griefs are much as baseless. As if,' he added, 'as if there were any real grief in the world,—except the gout!'

'He is like Obermann, like Amiel,' she said timidly. She had read passages in the volumes of those dreamy and isolated thinkers in the library of Amyôt. Friederich Othmar shrugged his shoulders; those names signified to him the very lowest deeps of human ineptitude and folly.

'Men who were so afraid of disappointment and disillusion that they would allow themselves to enjoy nothing! It would be as reasonable to let oneself die of starvation as a preventive of dyspepsia! Such men do not think; they only moon. The cattle that lie and graze under the trees have meditations quite as useful. My child,' he added, 'would you be wise or foolish if you threw all your diamonds into the river in anger because they were not stars? That is what your husband does with his life. You must learn to persuade him that the stars are unattainable, and that the diamonds represent a very fair and fruitful kingdom if not the powers of the air.'

Yseulte sighed wistfully. She vaguely felt that it was not within her means to reconcile him with the world and fate; she had not the magic wand.

'I am always in dread,' continued the Baron, 'that you, with your religious ideas, and he, with his impatience of his position, will do something extraordinary and Quixotic; will turn S. Pharamond into a *maison de santé*, or this hotel into a lazar-house for cancer. I shall never be surprised at any madness of that sort.'

Yseulte sighed a little.

'But, there is the misery of the world all around us,' she ventured to say; 'if we could alleviate it, would it not be worth any sacrifice?'

'My dear,' said Baron Fritz, 'when Napoléon gave the opium at Jaffa, he did more to alleviate suffering than all the philanthropists have ever done. Yet it has been always brought against him as his worst action. I went once, out of curiosity, to see the Incurables at the hospital of la Salpêtrière. Well, if false sentiment did not prevent the treatment à la Jaffa taking place there, an infinitude of hideous suffering and of hideous deformity would be mercifully nded. But the world is so sentimental that it will send several hundred thousand of young and healthy men to endure all kinds of tortures in war for a question of frontier, or a matter of national etiquette, but it esteems it unlawful to kill idiots or drug to death incurables cursed with elephantiasis or leprosy.'

Yseulte's clear eyes grew troubled; these views of life were perplexing to her. At Faïel all such contradictions had been simply accepted as ordained under one unquestioned and divine law; the conversation of Friederich Othmar depressed and bewildered her, but she could perceive its reason. It made her reflect; it made her more of a woman, less of a child. He thought that was for the best. If she were not educated in some worldly knowledge, the world would make an easy prey of her.

'Otho treats her as if she were an ivory madonnina who would remain aloof on an altar all her days,' he said to a woman he knew. 'On the contrary, she is a beautiful creature, about whom all the world will buzz and sting like bees about a lily. She must be taught not to throw away her honey. She is just now in the clouds; she is very much in love with a man who is not in love with her; she is full of ideals and impossible sentiments. She is half a child, half an angel; but to hold her own in the world she must be something else—not so angelic and not so childish,—and she must learn to esteem people at their value, which is for the most part very small. It would be even well if she could see Otho as he is; she would take life more easily. She would not be so likely to fall headlong from a heaven of adoration into a stone well of disillusion. Truths live at the bottom of these wells, no doubt, but they are not agreeable, and they give a shock to sensitive people. A woman is prettier when she is sensitive. It is like piety or charity—it is an essentially feminine ornament, but it is not a quality which wears well.'

His friend laughed.

'Do you think Othmar will thank you for so educating his wife?'

'He has never thanked me for anything that I have done,' he replied. 'But that does not prevent me from doing what I consider is my duty, or is most wise.'

'Say wisdom,' returned the lady. 'That suits you better than duty. Duty is ridiculous if you do not let *le bon Dieu* pose behind it.'

'I know people say so,' answered the Baron; 'but it is only an idea. In practical life agnostics and disbelievers of every sort make just as good citizens as the pietists.'

With the second week of December there was a great social event in Paris. The Hôtel Othmar was opened to the world. 'The gates of Janus unclose,' said one who deemed himself a wit in allusion to a war, then in embryo, into whose conception and gestation the gold of the Othmar was considered to enter largely.

The Boulevard S. Germain and all its approaches were like rivers of light, and the sound of carriage wheels was like the roll of artillery. 'Tout Paris' flocked there, and even the Faubourg disdained not to pass through those immense gates of gilded bronze, which were nicknamed of Janus, since the mistress of the salons within was by birth incontestibly a Comtesse de Valogne.

'Tiens, tiens, tiens!' murmured Aurore de Vannes. 'Is it possible for twelve months to have so changed a *fillette* into a goddess! Really, we were all wrong, and Othmar was right. We all thought her a *pauvrette*, to be put away in a holy house; he had the sense to see that she would become superb, and would set him right with all the Faubourg. The Faubourg was always well inclined to him, because his grandmother was a de Soissons-Valette, but his marriage has made him one of them: he is definitely placed for ever. Really, I never gave him credit for so much foresight when he sent that ivory casket. I thought it was only a caprice.'

'Othmar cares not a straw for the Faubourg,' said her husband, out of the pure spirit of contradiction. 'He will never give his millions to carry on a Holy War or restore the throne. He is more likely to dream of a great Western empire with its capital at the Golden Horn. He is a Slavophile.'

'He is wholly indifferent to politics; it is Baron Fritz who is the political conspirator,' returned the Duchesse. 'Otho is a mere dreamer, and he used to be a discontented one. Perhaps he is not so now.'

'He does not look especially happy; she does. I confess I should be sorry for him to become contented; the contemplation of his discontent has always reconciled me with having nothing myself,' said a great diplomatist, whose debts were as considerable as his talents.

'If he be not contented——' began the Duc, and paused, conscious that for him to say anything except a jest of any marriage under the sun would appear supremely ridiculous to his companions. Yet his admiration for Yseulte was not dormant, and took a still warmer character as he saw her in the *grande tenue* of a woman of the world, with the Othmar diamonds, long famous and long unseen, on her fair hair and her white breast.

'She has too many jewels for such a child,' he said irritably. 'She is covered with them like an Indian idol. That is so like a financier's love of display!'

'I dare say he has given them to her as you give toys to a child,' replied the diplomatist. 'Othmar has no faults of display. What has been almost ridiculous in him has been a simplicity of taste not in accord with his millions. But his wife is so very handsome that she may well betray him into some vanities.'

Twelve months had truly made in her that almost magical transformation which passion can cause in a very young and innocent girl who, from entire seclusion and absolute ignorance, is suddenly thrown into the arms of a man whom she has scarcely seen, yet timidly adores. She had lost her extreme spirituality of expression, but she had gained a thousand-fold in other ways. Her form had developed, her whole person had become that of a woman instead of a child; she was many years older than she had been one short year before, when, in her little quiet chamber under the woods of Faïel, she had only thought of love as a mystical religious emotion, and of herself as the betrothed of Christ.

She filled her place, and did the honours of her house with a calm grace which had nothing of the hesitation or the awkwardness of youth. He had told her what to do, and she did it with perfect ease, and that dignity which had so become her when she had curtsied to Melville as a little child in the old, dusky house in the Ile Saint-Louis. In manner she might have been a Queen of France for five-and-twenty years. It was only in the unworn transparency of the fair skin, beneath which the blood came and went so warmly, the slenderness of the lines of her form, the childlike naïveté of her smile, that her exceeding youthfulness was still revealed.

She made no single error; she said little, but she said always what was needful and becoming; she received each one of her guests with the phrase that pleased them, with the observances that were due to them; there was no hesitation or awkwardness in her. Even women who watched her, as her cousin did, with a malicious wish to find her at fault somewhere, were forced to confess to themselves that she bore herself admirably. If she had a defect, it was that she appeared a little cold. She was always exquisitely courteous; she was never familiar.

'She has the manner of the last century,' said Madame de Vannes, 'of the last century, before the women of Marie Antoinette rode donkeys and milked cows.'

To see that baby who six months ago had never spoken to any man except her confessor, and never worn any ornament except her convent medal, receiving sovereigns and princes and ambassadors, *de puissance à puissance*, and wearing diamonds which were ten times bigger, finer, and in greater profusion than her own, made her very angry, and yet made her laugh. She had seen many transformations of *fillettes* into great ladies, but none quite so rapid, so striking, or so complete as that of her young cousin into the mistress of the Hôtel Othmar.

'I wish Nadine Napraxine were here this evening,' she thought with that good-humoured malice which enjoys a friend's annoyance without meaning any real unkindness.

'All Paris will talk of your ball and much more of you to-morrow,' said de Vannes during the evening to his wife's cousin. 'Does that please you as much as it pleases most of them?'

'I shall not think about it,' replied Yseulte, simply.

'But I imagine you read the journals?'

'No, never.'

'Never!' he echoed, incredulously. 'Why is that?'

She hesitated, then answered with a little blush: 'He has told me not; he thinks they are foolish.'

'Othmar?' asked the Duc, with a laugh. 'Do you obey him as you did the Mother Superior?'

'Why not?' said Yseulte gently, but coldly.

'Why not!' he said irritably. 'Well, because you should begin as you wish to go on; you will not care for that state of servitude long; it would be better never to accustom him to it.'

'Excuse me, my cousin, I see Madame de Tavernes is looking for me,' said Yseulte, as she went to speak with a Duchesse whose genealogical tree mounted to the remote ages before the long-haired kings; a stately and powdered person who had issued from the retirement in which she usually lived to honour the first great entertainment of the daughter of Gui de Valogne.

The Duc was rebuffed and annoyed.

'She has learned her *riposte* already,' he thought, 'and she has not forgotten the locket. I wonder if he care? If he want to be free himself, he had better put her on a course of *petits journaux* at once. There is no recipe like that for corrupting the mind and debasing the taste. How handsome she is! What a lovely face—what a lovely form!—and only seventeen even now! She will be in perfect beauty for the next ten years. If he be not a very ardent or a very assiduous husband, he will not be able to keep all that to himself; he will have many rivals, and he will be sure to be unfaithful himself:—then she will read the journals and learn how women console themselves.'

At five o'clock that morning her rooms were empty, her guests were gone, and her woman had undressed her, and put on her a *négligée* of white silk; her hair was unloosened and fell behind her like a cascade of gold; all the great jewels were strewn on the table near; she was looking at her own reflection in the large oval silver-framed mirror before her; she smiled a little as she did so; her eyes were luminous, her cheeks were flushed; she was sensible of no fatigue, she was only elated with her own triumphs. She had had a girlish pleasure in receiving her cousins in that magnificent house; she had had an innocent triumph in showing how well she could fill the part of a woman of the world; she felt like a child who has played a queen's part in some pageant, and played it well; something of the insidious charm of the world had begun to steal on her; something of its vanity and of its rivalry had begun to attract her;—very little, for her nature was too proud, too pure, and too serious to yield easily to these temptations, but something nevertheless. Only as yet her one dominant thought was of him in it all. Had he also been content; had there been nothing that he could have desired otherwise?

She turned with a smile, half timid still, as he knocked at the door and entered her chamber. Her attendants withdrew at a sign from him; he took her in his arms and kissed her.

'I thank you for all your triumphs, dear,' he said kindly. 'They are mine.'

'Did I really do well?' she said doubtfully, but joyfully.

'Perfectly, perhaps almost too well; Paris will talk too much of you.'

'I forgot nothing?' she asked, still anxiously.

'You forgot nothing, and you looked—much too beautiful for men quickly to forgive me! No, dear, I do not flatter you; flattery would be absurd from me to you; I tell you the simple truth.'

'I am glad,' she said simply, 'for I have nothing else to reward you with for all you have given to me.'

She spoke shyly, for she was always in awe of him a little. Her arm, uncovered to the shoulder as the loose folds of the sleeve fell away from it, stole timidly about his throat; in all her caresses there was the hesitation of a proud and delicate nature blent with the longing of an ardent love. Habit had not familiarised her with the relation in which he stood to her; the brutalising intimacy of marriage had not dwarfed or dulled her ideal and adoration of him. He was still much less her lover than her lord.

Othmar took the bright gold of her heavy hair in his hand, and drew it through his fingers.

'On chasse de race,' he said, with a smile. 'You receive a great crowd as if you had been reared in a court from your babyhood.'

'You told me what to do,' she answered simply. 'It seems very easy; besides, every one was so extremely kind.'

'The kindness of society,' thought Othmar, 'the kiss of Judas!'

But he did not say so. Let her learn for herself what it was worth, he thought; the knowledge would come soon enough of itself.

Yseulte's face grew grave as she sat lost in thought.

'I do not think it is right to care for this sort of thing,' she said, with hesitation. 'It is only a sort of vanity. And then all these diamonds and these great pearls—they say they are worth millions—I do not like to wear them whilst there are so many without clothes or food of any kind; one knows that there is so much misery all about us here in Paris. Is it right, do you think, to enjoy oneself in this kind of way? I seem to remember nothing but myself all the day long——'

Othmar smiled and sighed.

'Enjoy, my child, while you can; leave all those grave thoughts for your older years. If you like to sell your jewels, and give them all to the poor, you can do it, but wait a few years first; wait to see more of the world. There is a cruel science, called political economy, which they certainly did not teach you at Faïel; you must learn something of that before you try to decide these questions, which have vainly perplexed every thoughtful man since rich and poor were together on earth. And now, shut your pretty eyes, and sleep and dream of your triumphs; they have been very innocent ones, you need not repent them.'

He kissed her again, and left her to her daybreak slumber in the warm orange-flower-scented air of her bed-chamber; and himself went out into the chill half-frozen streets of Paris on one of those errands of mercy of which he never spoke to any human being, and which were the result of his pity for men rather than of any belief or faith or sympathy that he had with them. He was one of the few men whom the lawless classes of Paris have ever respected.

Othmar himself could go unharmed where the police would not have ventured to go save in force; and in the days of the Commune the worst leaders of it had put a white cross on the great houses of which he was master, and spared them from torch and shell for sake of the young man who was wont to pass through the vilest quarters of Paris, with his hand ever open and his compassion never denied. They knew that if their *couches sociales* could have been an accomplished fact, Othmar himself would never have wished the old state of things maintained, but would have accepted the new with indifference and perfect courage, himself glad to be rid of a burden.

They forgave him his riches for sake of his own contempt for them; his courage, even his coldness, attracted them. He had no *blague*; he was entirely sincere; he never attempted to convert them to anything; he aided them without putting any price on his aid, either of gratitude or doctrine. They knew that he had neither fear of them nor love for them, but that he had a profound sense of a common humanity with them, which was in his eyes as in theirs another name for a common misfortune.

The times were out of joint for him. If he had been created with the capacity of religious faith, he would have been willingly what François Xavier or Père Lacordaire were. But he had the clear and critical intelligence of a man of the world; the fables of faith could not give him any mental pabulum. He took refuge in pity; it seemed to him that men were bound to do for one another at least as much as buffaloes do, which in trouble gather around the wounded ones of the herd.

Melville alone had found out something of what he did; Melville, who although the sweetest-voiced, softest-handed, of churchmen and courtiers in salon and boudoir, never feared or failed to descend into the haunts of iniquity, to grapple with disease and crime. In such places he and Othmar had met by chance more than once, and on one occasion Melville had said to him: 'You have more influence than I, because they do not suspect you; a priest is always suspected of trying to save souls only to serve his own.'

'If I have more influence than you, they are thankless,' rejoined Othmar; 'for you certainly love them, and I care nothing for them, absolutely nothing.'

'Why do you serve them, then?' asked Melville, in surprise.

Othmar sighed impatiently. 'It seems to me that one is bound in honour when fate has placed oneself beyond temptation;—besides, these reeking breeding-pens of crime in the midst of our own luxury are horrible; they are cancers in the very womb of human nature. Your Christianity has endeavoured to cure them for eighteen centuries, and has always failed miserably. The cancer grows and grows.'

Few persons save those of the police, who were perforce acquainted with his movements, were aware of the intimacy and influence he had acquired with the most wretched and the most dangerous classes of Paris; the food of *maisons centrales* and the emigrants of Nouméa. Often Friederich Othmar wondered within himself whither went the large sums which his nephew drew and spent without explanation; what he spent on art and on pleasure was known, but there were often great quantities of money taken by Othmar, in the exercise of his unquestionable right, for the use of which all the Baron's ingenuity failed to find an account. Numberless families redeemed from misery, many youths saved from crime and the galleys, many grown men aided to begin new lives in other climes, and many a foul place purged to moral and physical cleanliness, swallowed up these millions of francs, of which the employment remained a secret to the argus-eyes of Baron Fritz. There was a nobility about the indifference of this very rich man to his riches which conquered the hatred of the poor even amongst the Socialistic arrondissements, where such hatred was the sole religion recognised. They knew that Othmar himself was as disdainful of existent society as they were themselves, and that although fortune had so favoured him, he was no more content with the arrangement of the world than they were themselves. They were continually, brutally, ungrateful, but underneath their gratitude they liked him, and would never have harmed him.

As he walked out now into the misty air of dawn, he recalled the lovely face, with its sleepy eyelids, of his young wife with a sharp pang of conscience. Why could he not be content with that innocent and undivided love?

He recalled with a sense of some great fault in himself how entirely she was outside his life, how little hold she had upon his passions or his emotions. She was exquisite, she was purity itself in body and soul; he realised his own absolute possession of her as he had never done that of any other woman. He had been, that night, proud of her grace before the world, charmed by her manner, conscious of her incomparable distinction; and she was his as entirely as any flower that he might gather in a field. For him had been her first flush, her first kiss, her first consciousness of love; and yet, as he walked through the streets of Paris, leaving her to sink to sleep like a happy and tired child, he was conscious that his heart was indifferent to her; that, the mere early inclinations of the senses pacified, she had no power to rouse in him more than the kindly and indulgent affection which a child might have called forth by its helplessness and beauty.

He desired earnestly to make her as happy as any creature could be on earth, and would have denied her nothing which could have helped to make her so; but he could not command his own passions, and he could not make her the supreme mistress of them. She was a most lovely and most innocent creature, who was welcome to enjoy all the greatness and the grace of life with which he could dower her; she was a young saint who would bear his children in her breast as innocently as the peach-blossom bears the fruit; she was at all times both dear to him and sacred to him; but love for her was not there. He sighed impatiently as he felt that in all his words and his caresses he acted a part with her, that perhaps sooner or later, when the world had taught her better what men were, she would know that, and would be no longer so easily deceived.

As he had watched her that evening in her serenity, her gracefulness, her dignity, he had all at once remembered that in the great world youth grows rapidly, as a flower in a hothouse, that she would be surrounded by many who would ask no happier task than to enlighten her ignorance and embitter her confidence, and that if she ever came to learn and realise that she had owed her marriage partially to his compassion, and more still to his passion for another woman, her heart might break under the burden of that bitter knowledge, but her pride would never pardon the offence.

He began to feel as if he wronged her, though neither by act nor word had he been untrue to her since her marriage. She was so charming in every way, so delicate of thought, so graceful in expression, so intelligent even in her ignorance, so wholly worthy to inspire and retain the greatest love of a man's life, that he felt guilty before her, knowing that his pulses beat no quicker when he joined her after absence, that when her young lips, fresh as roses, touched his own, he met them without ardour or emotion. He had wished society to attract her; it seemed to him the quickest and the easiest compensation that he could offer her. At the root of the willingness with which he entertained the world, he to whom it was as indifferent as it was commonplace, was the unacknowledged sentiment that if Yseulte placed her happiness, as her temperament would lead her to do, in the inner life, in the affections and in the sympathies, she would be inevitably most miserable soon or late, since soon or late she would discover the poverty of his own heart; and his heart was richly endowed enough by nature to make him ashamed to think that it might ever be so. Friederich Othmar judged him harshly but justly; his indulgence and tenderness to her were not those of a lover, but were the accumulated gifts with which he strove to make her blind to his own coldness. The more he lived with her, the more he felt as though it were an unpardonable sin to have no love to give her, and the farther the possibility of such love receded from him. Esteem, admiration, tenderness, even affection, may all exist only to make the absence of love itself the more conspicuous.

As he went through the quiet streets, almost wholly deserted in the early hour of the morning, and swept by a keen wind, a waggon thundering along at too rapid a pace for so clumsy a vehicle caught the wheel of a carriage, which was coming in the opposite direction. The shock flung the carriage on the kerbstone; one of its two horses fell, the other struggled like a demoniac; the coachman and servant were thrown to the ground. Othmar naturally hastened to the spot. He was the only person in sight. The carriage itself had oscillated violently, but was not upset; its occupant had opened the door of it before he could arrive at the spot, and had leaped lightly out, though wrapped in sable furs from head to foot. When he reached the place, the fur-clad figure was standing in calm contemplation of the harm which had been done, and of the struggling horses which the coachman, who had sprung to his feet, was endeavouring to pacify.

'Othmar, is it you?' said a voice whose clear and sweet vibration sent the blood to his temples; and the eyes of Nadine Napraxine looked at him from under the sable lining of her velvet hood.

The waggon had blundered on out of sight, its driver in terror of the distant figure of a sergeant-de-ville who had now approached the scene. The fallen men had both found their feet, and the horses were still throwing themselves from side to side with broken traces and slippery pavement adding to the difficulty increased by their terror.

Othmar's own *coupé*, which followed him at a distance, had now come up, and his servants assisted hers. He opened the door of his own carriage.

'Pray accept it,' he said hurriedly. 'They will drive you where you wish; I will stay and help your people.'

'My people are idiots,' she said, as she gave them a disdainful glance. 'The waggon was large enough to be seen. I was coming from the Gare du Nord; my women and the *fourgons* are behind me. What are you about at this hour? Does the Countess Othmar allow you to be out so early—or so late?'

There was a grain of malice in the accent of the words; Othmar coloured despite himself, yet knew not why. He felt his whole being thrill at the mere sound of the sweet, cruel, well-remembered tones, and hated her.

She looked at him as they stood together on the kerbstone of the deserted and foggy street. She was enveloped in her long fur mantle, and none of the lines of her figure were traceable: she had no more contour than an

Esquimaux. Yet, nevertheless, that incomparable grace which belonged to her—as its movement to a bird, as its fragrance to a flower—seemed to detach itself, and escape, even from the heavy shapeless covering of the travelling-cloak in which she had been wrapped throughout her long express journey from Russia hither by way of Berlin and Strasburg. There was nothing visible of her except her starry eyes, and yet all the irresistible power which she possessed made his pulses fast and his thought confused; he strove against his own weakness, and pressed his offer on her with a cold courtesy.

'Well, I will take it since you wish it,' she said, as she entered his *coupé*. 'You will say who I am to this sergeant-de-ville, and whatever else may be necessary, though it is no case for the police since the waggoner has made good his escape; and if he had not, I certainly should let him alone. Tell your men my address—you remember it? *Au revoir!* I shall come and witness your happiness. Many things from me to your wife.'

They were only the usual words of commonplace politeness, yet to the ear of Othmar they were fraught with a thousand meanings. 'C'est le ton qui fait la musique,' and the tone of these perfectly simple sentences had for him irony, mockery, menace, and ridicule. Remember her address! Remember the Hôtel Napraxine! As if to his dying day he would ever forget the slightest trifle which had ever been associated with her!

His horses started off at a swift trot, and he lost her from sight. The questions of the police as to the cause of the accident started him as though someone had spoken to him in his sleep. When the matter was over, and the disabled carriage had been dragged away by hand, and the frightened horses led homewards by their coachman, it was too late to go where he had intended. He returned to his own house, bathed, dressed, and went to his library; but he could not give his attention to what he read. Nor when, with the early hours of the forenoon, various persons came to see him by appointment, could he confine his thoughts to the subjects under consideration.

At noon he gave his card to a servant, and told the man to go and inquire at her hotel if the Princess Napraxine had suffered any inconvenience from the accident of that morning.

The servant brought him back one of the small pale-rose-tinted notes, folded in three, with the crown embossed in silver, which he knew so well. The few lines in it said only:

'Merci bien. Vous êtes toujours preux chevalier. Je n'ai rien souffert du tout. Le Prince vous remerciera.—N. N.'

It was the merest trifle, a thing of no import, such as she wrote by scores every week to numbers of indifferent people; yet it had a sort of fascination for him. He could not destroy it; its faint subtle scent, like that of a tea-rose, recalled so vividly the charm of the woman who had written it; it seemed to him as if no one but Nadine Napraxine could have sent that little note, coloured like a sea-shell, delicate as a butterfly, with its miniature and *mignonne* writing. Ashamed of his own weakness, and angry with himself for his own concessions, he threw it into a drawer of his bureau and turned the key on it.

He had not seen her for a year, and her spell was unbroken; all he had done to escape from it was of no avail. One glance of her eyes from beneath the furs in that bleak, grey, misty daybreak, had sufficed to re-establish her dominion. He was conscious that life seemed no more the same to him since that chance encounter; it would be more troubled, more excited, more disturbed, but it would not be again the dull and even course which it had seemed to be when he had entered absent from her.

'I will never see her, except in a crowd,' he said to himself, whilst he remembered, with self-reproach, the tender caresses of Yseulte, which left him so calm, and even in his heart so cold!

Of course he had known that the Princess Napraxine, who was more Parisienne than the Parisiennes, would, sooner or later, return to her home there; would sooner or later reappear in the society which she had always preferred to all other. Russia had never held her long, and the seclusion which both her taste and her irritation had made her seek after the suicide of Seliedoff could not, in the nature of things, have lasted longer than one season. Yet the sense that she was there within a few streets of him, separated only by a few roods of house-roof from him, affected him with a force altogether unforeseen. He realised in it that there is no cure in simples for strong fevers, and that the will of a man is as naught against the dominion of passion. Even that slight letter, with its odour as of pale rose-buds, had a power over him which all the loveliness and innocence of Yseulte could not exercise. The irresistible force of his own emotions humiliated him in his own eyes.

He shrank a little, with almost a sense of guiltiness, as a little tap came on the panels of the library door, and from behind the tapestry the fair head of his young wife peeped cautiously.

'May I come in?' she asked, as a child might have done.

He rose with instinctive courtesy and opened the door to her.

It was noonday, and her few hours of sleep had sufficed to banish all her fatigue, and to make her as fresh, as radiant, and as clear-eyed, as she had been in the summer woods of Amyôt. She had none of the languor which late hours cause in later years; she had slept as soundly as a young fawn tired with its play, and had awakened as refreshed as a flower that uncloses at sunrise. She wore a long loose gown of palest blue, opening a little at the throat, with much old lace, of which the yellow tinge made whiter still the whiteness of her skin. The gown was of satin, and had gleams and shadows in it as she moved. Her eyes smiled; her cheeks were flushed from her bath; her entrance had a childish eagerness.

'Do tell me again that I did well last night,' she said, with a child's longing for the recapitulation of its innocent triumphs.

He did not look at her as he drew her to him with a mechanical caress.

'You did perfectly,' he answered, absently. 'A great ball is a woman's Austerlitz, I suppose. Do not let it make you in love with the world.'

'One cannot but like it,' she said, with her habitual truthfulness, a little wistfully. 'That is what I thought last night; perhaps it is wrong—when so many suffer——'

'They would not suffer a whit less if you did not give a ball.'

She hesitated, being still shy with him, and afraid of that which she had never seen, but which she always dreaded, his displeasure.

'But,' she said timidly, 'when one *is* so very happy, one wants to do something to deserve it. You have made for me such a perfect life, I want to give others something out of it. I should like to be useful, to show that I am grateful; not only to give away money——'

She paused, colouring a little at her own temerity. She did not express herself very well, because she was so much in earnest, and so uncertain as to whether it would seem discontented or vain in her to say so much. In an earlier moment the words would have touched his heart; he would have probably replied by admitting her into some association with the efforts of his own life, and some knowledge of his own desires and regrets for humanity at large. But in that instant he was only anxious to be alone. He answered a little absently:

'My child, ask your confessor these questions; he will show you many ways; you think him a good man—I have too many doubts myself to be able to solve yours.'

He spoke with a certain impatience; the harsher note grated on her sensitive ear. She felt that her scruples, which were very honest and sincere, did not meet with the same sympathy from him that they had received a few hours earlier.

A shadow passed over her face and she was silent.

'My dear,' continued Othmar, a little penitently, a little inconsistently, 'I have had such doubts as yours all my life, but no one has ever respected me for them; not even those in whose interest they tormented me. We cannot be wiser than all the world. If we stripped ourselves bare to found some community or some universal asylum, we should only be ridiculed as visionaries or as mischievous disturbers of the public peace and of the balance of fortune. Charity has oftener created a proletariat than it has increased prosperity. These questions have haunted me all my life. When I have found an answer to them, I will tell you. Until then, enjoy yourself. You are at the age when enjoyment is most possible and most natural. I wish your days to be happy.'

He spoke with a certain distraction; he was thinking little of what he said, much of the eyes which had looked at him from under the gloom of the fur in the mists of the dawn. He sighed unconsciously as he felt that this innocent young life beside him was no more to him—hardly more—than the flower which she wore at her throat. He recognised all its beauty, spiritual and physical, but only as he might have done that of a picture he looked at, of a poem he read.

'Enjoy yourself, dear; why not?' he added with kindness. 'You were made to smile as a primrose is made to blossom, and it is now mid-April with you.'

He kissed her, and passed his hand carelessly over her hair, then he glanced at the clock on his writing-table.

'I must leave you, for I have an appointment to keep. What are you going to do with your day?'

'Blanchette is to come to me. I have not seen her yet. The children are only now up from Bois le Roy, and Toinon is ill.'

She answered him with a little sigh. She wanted him to understand, and she could not better explain, how her own intense thankfulness for the new joys of her life filled her sensitive conscience with a trembling longing to become more worthy of it all, and to let the light which was about her stream into all dark places, and illumine them with love and peace. But she felt chilled, and discouraged, and silenced; and she had been so accustomed to keep all rebellious thoughts mute, that she did not dream of pursuing a theme to which he appeared indifferent. He kissed her hand and left her. She sank down for a moment on the writing-chair he had occupied before the table, and leaned her forehead on her hands with the first vague sensation of loneliness which had ever touched her since her marriage day.

'If my little child had been born alive,' she thought, 'then I should always have known what duty to do, what use to be——'

It was an infinite trouble to her conscience that in these great palaces of the Othmars she was as useless in her own sight as any one of the green palm trees or the rose-hued parrots in the conservatories. She could give money away, indeed,—almost endlessly; but that did not seem enough to do; that counted to her as nothing, for it cost no effort. It hurt her to feel, as she did feel vaguely, that she was no more the companion of her husband than the marble statue of Athene which stood at one end of his great library. He was infinitely indulgent to her. He was perfectly courteous and kind, and generous even to excess; but he never opened his heart to her, he never made her those familiar confidences which are the sweetest homage that a man can render to a woman, even when they display his own weakness or unwisdom. She had too little experience to be able to measure all that this meant, all of which it argued the absence; but as much perception as she had of it mortified her. At Amyôt she had vaguely suffered from it, but here, in Paris, he seemed very far away from her in thought and feeling. She felt that she was but one of the ornaments of his house, as the azaleas and palms were in their great porcelain vases.

To be exquisitely dressed, to be the possessor of some of the finest jewels in the world, to be told to amuse herself as she chose, to have the world at her feet, and all Paris look after her as she drove over its asphalte, would have been enough to most women of her age to make up perfect happiness; but it was not enough for the girl whose thoughtful years had been passed under the sad and solemn skies of Morbihan, and who had the sense of duty and the instincts of honour inherited from great races who had perished on the scaffold and on the battle-field. There was a pensive seriousness in her nature which would not permit her to abandon herself wholly to the self-indulgences and gaieties of the life of the world. She was too grave and too spiritual to become one of the butterflies who flirt with folly from noonday till night. Her chastened childhood in the darkened rooms on the Ile St. Louis had left a gravity with her which could not easily assimilate itself to the levity and the licence of modern society, which offended her taste as it affronted her delicacy.

CHAPTER XXXV.

A few minutes after Othmar had left the house her groom of the chambers ushered into the library the Duc de Vannes and his elder daughter. Blanchette, muffled up to her dancing turquoise-coloured eyes in sealskin, and with her small, impatient feet cased in little velvet boots lined with fur, in which costume Carlos Durand was about to paint her portrait for the salon, with a background of snow and frosted boughs taken from the Bois, sprang across the long room with the speed of a little greyhound, and embraced her cousin as if she had never loved anyone so much in all the days of her life. They had not met for six months, for Blanchette had been in penitence with her governesses and the dowager Duchesse de Vannes, in the depths of the Jura; a chastisement which had only sent her back to Paris two centimètres taller, full of resolution to avenge herself, and more open-eyed and quick-eared than ever.

'Ah, my dearest! How happy I am to see you again!' she cried in ecstasy, lifting her pretty little pale face to be kissed, in a transport of affection.

'Il faut la ménager: elle est si riche!' she had said to Toinon that morning, who was in bed with a cold, and who had grumbled in answer, 'Autrefois elle était si bête!' to which Blanchette had judiciously replied, 'On n'est jamais bête quand on est riche.'

De Vannes, when his little daughter's ecstasies were somewhat spent, approached with a smile and kissed the hand of Yseulte with a reverential but cousinly familiarity.

'Out so early!' she said in surprise. 'Surely you never used to see the outer air till two o'clock?'

'I brought this *feu-follet* to enjoy your kindness,' said the Duc, 'that I might have the pleasure of seeing you before all the world does. I wished, too, to be the first to congratulate you, my cousin, on your brilliant success last night. You were perfect, marvellous, incredible!——'

'I think I was much like any one else,' said Yseulte, to check the torrent of his adjectives; 'and the success of the ball was due more to Julien than to us; he was so enchanted to have a ball to organise in this great house after so many years without any receptions.'

'Julien is an admirable maître d'hôtel, no doubt,' answered de Vannes, with a smile; 'and he is happy in possessing a young mistress who appreciates his zeal and fidelity, but it is not of Julien that all Paris is talking and sighing this morning.'

'They must be talking and sighing in their beds then,' said Yseulte, a little impatiently. 'I thought no one was up so early as this except myself. Is the Duchesse well? She was so kind last night; she gave so much *entrain*——'

'You know I never see her till dinner, if then, unless I chance to cross her in the Bois,' answered the Duc, a little irritably.

He had risen three hours too early, and had bored himself to bring his little daughter here in his *coupé*; and he felt that so much self-sacrifice was not likely to avail him anything except that as he looked at Yseulte he could see for once in his life a woman who was still prettier in the morning than at night. He himself did not bear that trying light well; the lines about his eyes were deep and not to be hidden by any art, his eyes were dull and heavy, his cheeks hollow, and his moustache dyed. By night he was still one of the most elegant of *la haute gomme*, and his natural distinction could never altogether leave him; but his manner of life had aged him prematurely, and he felt old beside the freshness and the youth of Yseulte.

His vanity and his good sense alike counselled him to retire from a position which would avail him nothing; but a certain malice, which was a part of his character, and which his little daughter had inherited in increased degree, prompted him first to take reprisal for the indifference of his reception. Yseulte remained standing, holding the hand of Blanchette, evidently not desiring that he should be long there, and giving him no invitation to protract his visit until her breakfast hour. Blanchette's mischievous eyes watched her father's visible annoyance with keen appreciation of it; she had not forgotten the medallion given at Millo, and she had guessed very well why she had received the extraordinary honour of a seat in his brougham as he drove to the Jockey. She had been just about to leave the house with her maid when the Duc, passing her in the vestibule, had said carelessly: 'Is it you, you little cat? Ah, you are going to your cousin. Well, jump in with me, and I will set you down as I pass; I am going to the Jockey.' Now Blanchette knew as well as he did that the way from their house to the Jockey Club did not by any means lie past the Hôtel d'Othmar; but she had been too shrewd to say that, and too proud of driving beside her father, who smoked a big cheroot, and told her about the little theatres.

'Can I see Othmar?' he asked now, as he made his adieux to Yseulte.

'I am sorry, but he is just gone out,' she answered; 'I think he is gone for some hours; I do not know where.'

'You will soon learn not to say so,' thought the Duc, diverted even in his discomfiture by her simplicity. He said aloud:

'Do you think he may have gone to see the Napraxines? He was always a great friend of theirs, and they arrived last night; it is in all the papers, but then you do not read the papers. I only ask, because I should be so glad if I could meet him anywhere. The Prefect of Nice writes to me about the basin of Millo; now S. Pharamond has much more sea-front and much larger share of the harbour than we have, and if Othmar would use his influence, one word from him——'

'I will tell him; he will be sure to come to you or write to you,' she said quickly. She had flinched a little at the name of the Napraxine, which no one had spoken to her since that silver statue of the Love with the empty gourd had been sent to her before her marriage.

'Bien joué, petit papa,' thought Blanchette, with understanding and appreciation, as her father bowed himself out of Othmar's library.

'Oh, how happy you are!—how I wish I were you!' she cried, five minutes later, as she skipped about her cousin's boudoir, while the glow of the fire of olive-wood shone on the panels which Bougereau had painted there with groups of those charming nude children which he can set frolicking with almost the soft poetic grace of Correggio.

Yseulte smiled on the little impudent face of the child, who leaned her elbows on her knees as she spoke.

'I am very happy,' she said, with perfect truth. 'But I hope you will be as much so one day, Blanchette.'

Blanchette nodded.

'I shall marry into the finance too; the noblesse is finished; papa says so. He said yesterday, "Nous sommes de vieux bonzes—emballons-nous!"'

Blanchette tied her arms and legs in a knot as she had seen a clown do, and made a pantomimic show of being rolled away on a wheelbarrow; then she gathered herself up and came and stood before her cousin and hostess.

'Te voilà, grande dame!' she cried, looking at her with her own little pert flaxen head, with its innumerable little curls held on one side critically, as she surveyed Yseulte from head to foot with a frank astonishment and admiration. It was only such a little while ago that Yseulte had been her butt and victim at Millo; that she had ridiculed her for her grey convent dress, her thick shoes, her primitive, pious habits, brought from the Breton woods, and lo!—here she stood, 'très grande dame!' as Blanchette, a severe judge in such matters, acknowledged to herself. So tall, so elegant, so stately, with her beautiful slender hands covered with great rings, and her morning-gown a cascade of marvellous old lace. 'She looks quite twenty years old!' thought Blanchette. 'How nice it must be to be married, if one get grown up all at once like that!'

She was so absorbed in her thoughts that she was unusually quiet for a little time, during which her terrible eyes scanned every detail of Yseulte's appearance, from the pearl solitaire at her throat to the gold buckles in her shoes. Then, with a shriek of laughter, she cried aloud:

'Do you remember when you came first to us you had leather shoes— leather!—and no heels, and mamma sent you at once to have some proper shoes; and how you could not walk a step in them, and cried?'

'I remember,' said Yseulte good-humouredly, 'but I wonder you do—you were so little.'

'Oh, I never forget anything,' replied Blanchette, sagely. 'What beautiful feet you have now, and you are so grown, so grown! And I want to see all your jewels. Mamma says they are wonderful. I love jewels.'

'You shall see them, if you like, by-and-bye. But you did see many before my marriage.'

'But mamma says he has given you ever so many more since—that you were covered with them at your ball.'

'He is always generous.'

Yseulte smiled as she spoke—the dreamy introspective smile of one who recalls happy hours.

'*Tope-là*, while it lasts,' said the small cynic before her.

'Hush,' said Yseulte, with some disgust.

'Papa never gives mamma anything,' pursued Blanchette. 'Papa gives heaps of things to Mdlle. Fraise; the one they call Rose Fraise. She plays; she has eyes like saucers; she is at the Variétés; she rides a roan horse in the Bois of a morning. Don't you go to the theatre every night? When I marry I shall have a box at every house. I have gone to Hengler's. Now show me the jewels, will you?'

To humour the child, Yseulte took her to her dressing-room, where the tortoiseshell and silver box, which was the outer shell of the iron fire-proof jewel case, was kept, and told her women to open it. Blanchette remained in an almost religious ecstasy before the treasures exposed to her adoring eyes. Nothing could awe this true child of her century except such a display as she now saw of ropes of pearls, streams of sapphires, emeralds green as the deep sea, diamonds in all possible settings, rare Italian jewels of the Renaissance, and Byzantine and Persian work of the rarest quality. She was, after an hour's worship, with difficulty persuaded to leave the spot where such divine objects were shut within their silver shrine defended by Chubb's locks.

'You *are* happy!' she said, with a sigh.

Yseulte glanced at a miniature of Othmar which stood near.

'That is worth them all!' she said, and then coloured, vexed that she had betrayed herself to the artificial, satirical mockery of the child.

But Blanchette did not hear; she was thinking of the great diamonds lying like planets and comets fallen out of the sky into their velvet beds.

'*Dis donc,*' she said abruptly, 'what is your budget for your toilettes? You would not tell me when you married; tell me now.'

'I do not think it concerns you, my dear, and your mamma knows,' replied Yseulte.

'Oh, it made mamma very angry; she said he gave you three times as much as she has; that is why I want to know what it is, because then I should know what hers is. And I know she is in debt so deep!' and Blanchette held her little hand high above her head. 'What is the first thing you ordered, Yseulte? Me, I should order a petticoat with valenciennes quite up to the top; like that they are three thousand francs each. Yours are like that? You have got them in all colours, and ever so many white satin ones too? If I were you, I should be all day long with the *lingères* and *costumiers*. Are you not with them all day long?'

'No, I have ordered nothing; I want nothing; I have such quantities of clothes;—if I live to be a hundred I shall never wear them out!——'

'Wear them out!' cried Blanchette, with a scream which was as inimitable as a shriek of Judic's or Jeanne Granier's. 'What an expression! One would think you were a doctor's wife in the provinces. You know you can never wear anything more than three times, and a *toilette du soir* never but once. Your maids surely tell you that?——'

'I wear what they put out,' said Yseulte, a little amused. 'But I doubt very much whether I shall ever care about *chiffons*; not in your sense of caring, Blanchette. Of course I like pretty things, but there are so many other ways of spending money.'

'What ways?' said the child sharply. 'Play? Horses? The Bourse? Or do you buy big jewels? It is very safe to buy big jewels; you can run away with them in revolution, sown in your stays——'

'There is so much to do for the poor,' said Yseulte, with a little hesitation; she feared to seem to boast of her own charity, yet she thought it wrong to let the child think that she spent all she had selfishly and frivolously.

Blanchette's little rosy mouth grinned.

'For the poor? One can *quêter*, that is always amusing. I stood at the door of S. Philippe after Mass last month, and I got such a bagful of napoleons, and I wore a frock, *couleur de feu*, and a Henri-Trois hat, and Monseigneur himself kissed me—it was great fun—there was a crowd in the street, and one of them said, "'Est crâne, la pétiote!" It was a baker's boy said it; I threw him a napoleon out of the bag.'

'Oh, Blanchette!—out of the alms money!'

'Why not? I put a dragée in instead, and I dare say the boy was poor, or he wouldn't have had a basket on his head. Monseigneur said to mamma that I was one of the children of heaven!'

And Blanchette made her *pied de nez*, and waltzed round on one foot.

'You could buy the whole of Siraudin's and not feel it,' she resumed enviously. 'You could buy half Paris they say; why don't you?'

'I have all I want,' said Yseulte; 'very much more than I want.'

'That is nonsense; one need never stop wishing——'

'One must be very ungrateful then,' said Yseulte. 'But you can wish as much as you like this morning; you shall have your wishes. Only I should like to hear you wish that Toinon were with you. Poor Toinon, at home with her sore throat!'

'I don't wish that at all,' said Blanchette sturdily. 'She pinches, she gobbles, and *she* is vulgar, if you like; she swears like the grooms. You know our rooms overlook the stables; we can hear all the men say when they are cleaning the horses. Toinon makes signals to the English tiger Bob, and he to her. Toinon will only marry someone who keeps a fine *meute* and good colours for a hunting-dress. She only lives for the Cours Hippique. She got her sore throat because she would go on M. de Rochmont's break when it was raining.'

'Poor Toinon! You ought to be so fond of each other. If I had had a sister——'

'Ab-bah!' said Blanchette; 'you would have hated her! I can never have a scrap of pleasure in a new frock because Toinon always has one too; I know I do not make half the effect I should do if I were all alone!'

'Hush! If Toinon died, only think how sorry you would be!'

Blanchette laughed in silence; she did not dare to say so, but she thought that if Toinon did die it would be a bore in one way, because death always dressed one in black, and shut one up in the house; but otherwise—there were quantities of Toinon's things which she would like to possess herself, and in especial a set of pink coral, which Toinon's godmother, the Queen of Naples, had given her, which was delicious. Blanchette's own godmother was but little use to her, being a most religious and most rigid Marquise, who dwelt on her estates in a lonely part of La Vendée, and only made her presents of holy books and crucifixes and relics in little antique boxes.

'Do you know, Yseulte,' she continued, with her persistent prattle, as she hopped round the room, examining and appraising as accurately as a dealer at the Drouot the treasures which it contained, 'they make bets about you at the clubs? How nice that is! Nobody is anything in Paris till the clubs do that. Papa and the Marquis have a hundred thousand francs on it, and mamma laughs;—they think I don't hear these things, but I do.'

'Bets on me?' repeated Yseulte in wonder. 'Why should they bet about me?'

'Oh, they bet as to whether you will be the first to *flanquer* Count Othmar, or he you. They often make that sort of bet when people marry. Papa is all for you; he says you will be *flanquée*, and bear it like an angel,—"like a two-sous print of S. Marie!" said mamma.'

Yseulte coloured with natural indignation.

'You have no right to repeat such things if you hear them, Blanchette,' she said, with only a vague idea of the child's meaning. 'You might make great mischief. If Count Othmar were to know——'

'Bah!' said Blanchette. 'You will not tell him. You are in love with him; they all say so; it is what they laugh at: it is what they bet about—how long it will last, who will get him away first, what you will do, whether you will take some one else. Papa says you will not; mamma says you will: they quarrel ever so often about it. You see,' continued Blanchette, with her mixture of *blasé* cynicism and childish naïveté, which made her say the most horrible things with only a half perception of their meaning, 'they all only marry for that, to be able to take some one else; that is why it does not matter if one's husband is as old as the Pont Neuf and as ugly as Punch. You happen to be in love with your's, and he is handsome; but it only makes them laugh, and he was never in love with you—mamma says so; he married you because he was angry with Madame Napraxine, and he wanted to do something to vex her.'

Blanchette, who was given to such ruthless analysis of other people, did not dissect her own emotions, so that she was ignorant of the malice which actuated her speech, of the unconscious longing which moved her to put a thorn in the rose. She wanted all those jewels for herself! She knew very well she could not have them, that she would be laughed at by Toinon and everybody if it were known she wished for them; still, the longing for them made it pleasant to her to plant her little poisoned dagger in the happy breast of her cousin. But she paused, for once frightened at the sudden paleness of her cousin's face.

Yseulte gave a little low cry, like a wounded animal; she felt the air grow grey, the room go round her, for a moment, with the intensity of her surprise, the shock of her pain. But in another moment she recovered herself; she repulsed, almost without pausing to examine it, a suspicion which was an offence to himself and her. She laid her hand on the little gay figure of the cruel child, and stopped her in her airy circuit of the room, with a gesture so grave, a rebuke so calm, that even Blanchette was awed.

'My little cousin,' she said, with an authority and a serenity which seemed all at once to add a score of years to her age, 'you can jest with me, and at me, as much as ever you like, I shall forgive it and I shall never forget all I owed once to your mother; but if you venture to speak again of my husband without respect, I shall not forgive it. I shall close his house to you, and I shall tell your parents why I do so.'

Blanchette looked furtively up in her face, and understood that she was not to be trifled with. She began to whimper, and then to laugh, and then to murmur in the coaxing way she had when she had been most in fault.

'How grand you have grown, and how old in twelve months! You know I only talked nonsense; I never heard them say a word; I only wanted to teaze you; it is so silly, you see, Yseulte, to be so in love with M. Othmar, it is so bourgeoise and so stupid, and they all say that it is not the way to keep him. Me, when I marry, I will always make my husband call me Madame, and I will never let him touch but the tip of my little finger, and I will eat oysters every day, and drive the horse that wins the Grand Prix in my basket in the Bois. *Dis, donc!* you will not tell mamma I said anything naughty?'

'I shall not tell her,' said Yseulte, who could not so quickly smile. She felt as if some one had run a needle straight through her heart.

Blanchette laid her curly head against her cousin's breast:

'I do love you, Yseulte,' she murmured. 'You are always true, and you are always kind, and you are so handsome, so handsome! Mercié, and all the sculptors say so; and all the painters too. The Salon will be full of your busts and your portraits; Madame Napraxine is only a pale woman with great black eyes like coals in a figure of snow——'

'I desire you not to speak of Madame Napraxine!' said Yseulte, with a violence which startled herself and momentarily shook her self-control.

The child, who had ignorantly meant to atone and to console for her previous offence, was genuinely alarmed at her failure.

'I only meant that you are much prettier, much handsomer, than she is,' she stammered.

'Madame Napraxine's beauty is celebrated,' said Yseulte, with enforced calmness. 'Leave off your habit of indulging in personalities, Blanchette; it is a very vulgar fault, and it makes you malicious for the pleasure of fancying yourself witty. Come and feed my peacocks; they are birds who will recommend themselves to your esteem, for they are intensely vain, artificial, and egotistic; they believe flowers only grow that they may pull them to pieces.'

'I don't care for the peacocks,' said Blanchette. 'Drive me in the Bois in the *Daumont* with the four white horses, and you can buy me something at Siraudin's as we go.'

'As you like,' said Yseulte.

Yseulte humoured the child's caprices, and drove her out into the cold sparkling air with the four white horses, with their postilions in black velvet caps and jackets, which Blanchette condescended to praise as the most *chic* thing in all Paris. It was on the tip of her tongue to say that they were even more *chic* than the Napraxine black horses and Russian coachman, but she restrained herself, unwilling to offend her cousin before they stopped on their return from the Bois at Giroux's, at Siraudin's, and at Fontane's, for Blanchette was too sensible to be satisfied with toys and bonbons, and set her affections on three monkeys in silver-gilt, playing at see-saw on a tree trunk of jade, with little caps made of turquoises on their heads.

When she had chattered herself tired, and the day was declining, she consented to allow herself to be driven home, and Yseulte returned alone to the Boulevard S. Germain. For the first time since her marriage her heart was heavy. The selfishness and greed of her little companion were nothing new to her, but they had been made painfully evident in that drive through Paris; and the wound which the child had given her still smarted, as the bee-sting throbs after the insect has flown away. It was not that she believed what was said; she was too loyal and too innocently sure of her husband's affection to dishonour him by such suspicion. Yet the mere knowledge that such things were said of him and herself hurt her delicacy and her pride cruelly, and she knew well that, if the Duchesse de Vannes said so, then the world said so too. And her heart contracted as she thought involuntarily, 'Why should they speak of Madame Napraxine at all in connection with me, unless—unless he had loved her?'

Yseulte was too young to think with composure of the women who had preceded herself in the affections of her husband; she could not console herself, as older or colder women would have done, with the reflection that every man has many passions, and that the past should be a matter of indifference to one who was indissolubly united with his present and his future. To her it seemed that if he had ever loved any one else he could not care for her; all the ignorance and exaggeration of youth made this seem a certainty to her.

She was no longer the calm and innocent child that she had been at Millo; the passions of humanity had become to stir in her; love, the great creator and the great destroyer, had taken possession of her, and had roused in her impulses, jealousies, desires, of whose existence she had never dreamed; her temperament, naturally sweet and spiritual, had beneath it unknown springs of ardour and of passions: *le vin mousseux*, which her cousin Alain had said was latent in her blood from the impetuous and voluptuous race of her fathers. She could not wholly recover from the shock which she had received, as from a bolt that fell from sunny skies. It had been only a child's frothy foolish chatter, no doubt; yet the mere suggestion made in it clung to her memory with a cruel and terrible persistency. She did not doubt that the child had only repeated what she had heard; she knew that Blanchette's memory was as retentive as a telephone; and if the Duchesse de Vannes had said it, then the world had thought it. She had not allowed Blanchette to perceive the pain that she had caused; but as her horses had flashed through the chill bright frosty air of Paris, and the child's gay shrill voice had chattered incessantly beside her, she had suffered the first moments of anguish that she had known since her marriage. As she drove now through the streets of Paris, in which the lamps were beginning to sparkle through the red of the winter sunset, she felt a strange sense of solitude amidst those gay and hurrying crowds through which her postboys forced their fretting horses.

At Amyôt, on the days when Othmar had left her, she had never felt alone; she had amused herself with the dogs, the birds, the horses, the woods; she had dreamed over her classic music, or read some book which he had recommended, and spent hours looking from the balustrade of the great terrace, or from the embrasure of a window to watch for the first appearance in the avenue of the horses which should bring him from the station of Beaugency. She had never felt alone at Amyôt, but here in the city which she loved from the associations of childhood, and as the scene of her marriage, in this city which regarded her as one of the most fortunate of its favourites of fortune, she felt a sense of utter loneliness as the carriage rolled through the gates.

The *suisse* told her that Othmar had not come home.

She went upstairs to her boudoir and threw off her close-fitting-coat of sables and her sable hat, and sat down beside the olive-wood fire, drawing off her long gloves. The room was softly lighted with a rose-tinted light which shone on the gay children painted by Bougereau, the flowered satin of the curtains and couches, the Dresden frames of the mirrors, the marqueterie of the tables and consoles, the bouquets of roses of all growths and colours. She looked round it with a little sigh; with the same sense of chillness and sadness. Everything in it seemed to echo the cruel words: 'He only married you to anger her!'

In the morning the whole chamber had seemed to smile at her from all the thousand trifles, which spoke in it of his tender thoughtfulness for herself; now, the roses in their bowls, the children on their panels, the amorini holding up the mirrors, the green parrots swinging in their rings, all seemed to say with one voice, 'What if he never loved you?'

Her arms rested on her knees and her face on her hands, as she sat in a low chair before the fire which burned under white marble friezes of the Daphnephoria, carved by the hand of Clésinger. She could never ask him, she could never ask any one, of this cruel doubt, which had come into her perfect peace as a worm comes into a rose. All her pride shrank from the thought of laying bare such a wound. Not even in the confessional could she have brought herself to breathe a whisper of it. She was not yet seventeen years old, and she had already a doubt which, like the pains of maternity, she must shut in her heart and bear as best she might alone. She had both courage and resignation in her nature, and she needed both.

'It is impossible!' she murmured unconsciously, half aloud, as the memory of a thousand caresses and gestures, which seemed to her to be proof of the most absolute love, came to her thoughts with irresistible persuasion, and made her face grow warm with blushes even in her solitude. It was impossible that he did not love her—he who had been free to choose from the whole world.

'It is impossible!' she murmured, with her head lifted as though in some instinct of combat against some unseen foe.

'What is impossible?' said Othmar, as he entered the room and approached behind her, unseen until he had drawn her head backward and kissed her on the eyes. 'What is impossible, my child?' he repeated. 'No wish of yours if you tell it to me.'

She coloured very much, and rose, and remained silent. Her heart was beating fast; she did not know what to reply. By the light of the fire he did not see how red she grew and then how pale. He seated himself in a low chair and took her by the hand.

'What is so impossible,' he said carelessly, 'that you dream of it in my absence in the dark?'

'Nothing,—at least,—I would rather not say,' she murmured.

'As you like,' said Othmar. 'You know I am not Blue Beard, my dear.'

A great longing rushed through her to tell him what the Duchesse de Vannes had said, and ask him if it were true or false—he who alone could know the secrets of his own heart,—but sensitiveness, timidity, delicacy, pride, all made her mute. What use would it be to ask him? He would never wound her with the truth if the truth were what her cousin had said.

Othmar smiled kindly as he looked at her; she did not know that if he had loved her more he would have been more curious before this, her first secret, less willingly resigned to be shut out from her confidence.

'Who has been with you to-day?' he asked. 'Oh, I remember, you have had little Blanchette. What a terrible child; she is an Elzevir compendium of the century. Has she said anything to vex you? She is as malicious as Mascarille——'

Yseulte touched his hand timidly. There was a grain of fear in her adoration of him, that fear which enters into all great love, though Nadine Napraxine and Madame de Vannes would have ridiculed it as 'jeu de lac et de nacelle,' the 'vieux jeu' of the romanticists and sentimentalists.

'You do love me?' she said, very low, with much hesitation, while her colour deepened.

Othmar looked up quickly with a certain irritation.

'Has that pert baby told you to doubt it? Can that be a question between you and me? My dear child, would you be by me now if I did not do so?'

And he soothed her agitation by those caresses with which a man can so easily and with pleasure to himself counterfeit warmth and tenderness to a woman who has youth and grace and cheeks as soft as the wing of a bird.

'Yseulte,' he said gravely a few moments later, 'do not listen to what other women say to you; if you do, you will lose your beautiful serenity and fret yourself vainly by doubts and fancies. There is nothing on earth so cruel to a woman as women. They envy you—not for me—but for what you possess through me and for the face and form with which nature has dowered you. Do not let them poison your peace. I am not afraid that they will corrupt your heart, but I am afraid that they may distress and disturb you. We cannot live all our lives in seclusion at Amyôt, and the world must come about you soon or late. To be in the world means to be surrounded with jealousies, cruelties, enmities, ingratitude, and malice; if we once lend our ear to what these will tell us, we shall have no more happiness. You have been like your favourite, S. Ignace; by reason of your own purity you have been allowed to hear the angels sing. Do not let the world's clamour drown that divine song, for once lost no one ever hears it again! Do you understand what I mean, my dear?'

She said nothing, but she hid her face on his breast and burst into tears, the first that he had ever seen from her eyes.

'Can they not let her alone,' he thought with anger, and a sense of weariness and apprehension; if the world taught her what men's love could be, would she not discover what was missing in his?

CHAPTER XXXVI.

When the three black horses of the Princess Napraxine, with their manes flying in the wind, their eyes flashing, and their nostrils breathing fire, dashed down the Champs Elysées to make the tour du Bois, all Paris looked after her, and multitudes who only knew her by repute took off their hats to her as they had used to do in a bygone time to the golden-haired empress.

'Ah, if I had been in that woman's place in 'seventy-one,' she thought once, 'I would not have run away in a cab with Evans the dentist; I would have put on a white gown and all my diamonds, and gone out before them on to the terrace of the Tuileries—they would have forgotten Sedan, and would have worshipped me! I cannot forgive people who have the happiness of great opportunities for not rising to be equal to them. One can but die once, and it must be essentially delightful to die amidst a roll of drums, a blaze of sunset, a storm of welcome. The death of Desaix at Marengo is the ideal death.'

There was at the bottom of her soul, despite her languor, ennui, and pessimism, a certain heroic element; life seemed to her so poor a thing, so stupid, so illogical, that if it went out in fire it vindicated itself in a measure.

'Sometimes, do you know,' she said once to a sympathetic companion, 'I think I might have been something great if I had been born in the time for it; all depends upon that. Mdlle. de Sombreuil would have lived and died like ten thousand other Frenchwomen, in the monotony of the *vie de château*, if she had not happened to be alive under the Terror. What possibility of any greatness is there for a woman who lives nowadays in what calls itself the great world? The very men who have any genius in it are dwarfed by it. Modern life is so trivial, yet so absorbing; it is such a bed of down and such a bed of prickles; it is such a sleeping-potion and such a whip of nettles, that we have no time to think about anything but itself. You must live "à l'abri des hommes," if you want to be of higher stature than they are. Bismarck is a colossus, because he shuts himself up in Varzin so constantly. It is very hard even for men to resist the presence of the world; even Tennyson leaves Farringford in the primrose month to court a vulgar apotheosis in the London drawing-rooms; and for a woman who finds herself from birth upward in that *milieu* there is no resistance possible. We are born to dress, to drive, to dine, to dance, to set the fashion in all kinds of things,—and that is all. If we are clever, we do mischief in meddling with the hidden cards of diplomacy or statecraft, and if we are light-minded we do a different manner of mischief in making all sorts of vices look pretty and distinguished to those below us, who are always endeavouring to imitate us; but more than that we cannot do. The morphine has been injected into our veins; we cannot resist its influence; there is a kind of excitement and somnolence, both at once, in the routine of our world which none of us can resist. If we have any brains, perhaps we make resolutions to resist, but we do not keep them; the world we live in is idiotic but it is irresistible. When we wake, we see the heap of invitation cards on our table; we yawn, but we yield, and we fill up our book of engagements; the day is crowded, so is the year; and so life slips away hurried, tired, thinking itself amused. Sometimes I think I should like to live amongst the corn-fields and the larchwoods, and do good, and I dare say I shall when I am old, or, what is still worse than old, middle-aged. But you know one does not do good in that way; one always gets imposed on, and the Jew money-lender in the centre of the village would be really the person who would profit by one's charities. It is quite easy for stupid people to be happy; they believe in fables and they trot on in a beaten track like a horse on a tramway. But when you have some intelligence, and have read something besides your breviary, and have studied the philosophy of life a little, it is much more difficult to content yourself. My friends who are putting on blisters and bandages at the hospitals, fancy they are on the way to eternal salvation, but a political economist would tell them that they were only doing a vast deal of mischief, upsetting the nicely-balanced arrangements of Nature. Myself, I think, Nature has very little to do with the world as it is in the nineteenth century in Europe. I do not think Nature, left to herself, would create either cripples or cancers, any more than she would yoke bullocks or cut terriers' tails.'

She had accompanied her friends the Dames du Calvaire more than once to those hospitals, where patrician hands touched the leper's sores and the idiot's ulcers; but her delicate taste had been revolted, and her intelligence, nurtured on shrewd and satiric philosophies, had rejected the idea that any good was done by great ladies transforming themselves into sick nurses of disease. She thought it must be infinitely delightful to be able to delude yourself in that kind of way, to think that you pleased Deity by putting on a poultice and averted a social cataclysm by washing a cretin, but she did not believe in that kind of thing herself. She did not see how any one could do so who had thought about life, and the rest of it.

'I dare say I am quite useless,' she would reply to those who tried to convince her, 'but then so many things are. Who has ever found out the use of butterflies, or of daisies, or of a nautilus, or of a nightingale, or of those charming rosy clouds which drift about at sunset? I do not see the utility of prolonging the horrible and miserable lives of lepers and of idiots in hospitals and asylums. Humanity is not in the least served; it is much more often profoundly noxious and disgusting. Even the people who talk about its sanctity, do not believe in what they say, or war would become an impossibility, and so would all the factories which, as Victor Hugo has said, take the soul out of man to put it into machinery.'

When she spoke in this way she was very much in earnest, and her arguments were very hard to refute; and even Melville went out of her presence with an uncomfortable, though unacknowledged, sense that his whole life had been a mistake based on a bubble which had all the hues of the rainbow, indeed, but no more than a bubble's solidity. When the men of science, with whom she sometimes amused herself by playing the part of the great Catherine to the Encyclopædists, came into her presence, they fared no better than the priests, and she did not believe in them a whit the more.

'Five hundred years hence, your ideas and your discoveries will all be refuted and ridiculed,' she said to them, 'as you now refute and ridicule the physiology of the Greeks and Latins; you will not find the key to the mystery of creation by torturing dogs or chaining horses on a bed of agony.'

And she listened to them, but she laughed at them. To the satirical clearness of her highly-trained intelligence the delirium of science was quite as much a malady of the mind as were the rhapsodies of religion.

'La science est la grande névrose du moment; ça passera,' she said once to Claude Bernard.

In Paris, Nadine Napraxine was what the world had made her; she was the *élégante* of her period, a hothouse flower of fragile beauty, of absolute indolence, of hypercritical taste, of utter and entire uselessness. In her carriage or her sleigh, under her pile of silver fox skins; on a Tuesday at the Français, and on a Saturday at the Grand Opéra; on her Thursdays at her 'cinq heures,' when the most exclusive of crowds gathered in her drawing-rooms; in the few great assemblies and balls to which she deigned to carry her listless grace and her marvellous jewels; throughout her self-absorbed day, which began at noon and ended at dawn, she was a *cocodette* of the most exquisite grace and of the most incredible extravagance, such as Paris had known her to be from the second year of her marriage. Her caprices were unending, her changefulness was incalculable, her expenditure was enormous; the most exaggerated tales were told of her hauteur and of her exclusiveness, yet were not much beyond the truth; and men worshipped her, and women intrigued for her notice, just because she was so unapproachable and could be insolent. Fragile and white as the narcissus flower, which she always took as her emblem, with a voice ever sweet and low, and the most perfect manner in the world, she could be as cruel in all the cruelties of society as ever her ancestors had been with knout and steel in their frosty fastnesses. It amused her to see the timid recoil, the presumptuous shrink, the confident wither into humiliation, before the chillness of her smile, the terror of her few cold softly-spoken words.

'I am the only scavenger that Europe has left,' she said once. 'All the others have been frightened by the democracy, but I frighten the democracy, or, at least, I keep it out of my drawing-rooms. It may get into the "Almanac de Gotha," but it will not get past my *suisse* and up my staircase.'

Now and then she had been known to do exceedingly kind things, just as in the midst of her worldly life she would go now and then to a discourse at the Academy or to a séance at the Sorbonne. But they had been always done to persons quite simple and frank, who never affronted her with presumption or disgusted her with pretension. To a lie of any sort she was inexorable.

The Hôtel Napraxine was one of the most delightful houses in Europe. It stood near the entrance of the Avenue du Bois de Boulogne, and was withdrawn from every inquisitive glance which might be cast on it from the road, within gardens large enough to contain groves of lime trees and plane trees, fountains, lawns, pavilions, and terraces of rose-coloured marbles. No disturbing echo of the traffic of Paris could reach the sensitive ear of its sovereign lady when she sank to sleep under the white satin of her shell-shaped ivory bed.

All the finest French artists living had been summoned to its adornment within.

'All modern rooms are only like so many bonbon-boxes,' she had said. 'At least my bonbon-boxes shall be well-painted.'

And Meissonier, Duran, Baudry, Cabanel, Henner, Legros, had all signed some panel, some ceiling, some staircase, chimney-piece, or salon-wall in this most exquisite of houses.

'It is really charming,' she said to herself, when she reached it on that first grey, chill, misty morning of her arrival, and its delicious colour and warm air and flower-filled twilight welcomed her after the long dull journey across Europe. It was especially perfect to her this day because for some fifty hours at least her husband would not come thither. There was only one thing ever discordant in its perfect harmonies. When Platon Napraxine came up the staircase—with its black-and-white marbles, its pale-blue velvet carpets, its sculptures by Clésinger, and its wall-paintings by Baudry,—when he came up under the leaves of the bananas and the palms, and entered her own sanctuary, his broad tall form, his heavy step, his

Kalmuck face were dissonant and absurd in it all, and irritated her sense of fitness, and annoyed her like a false note in the middle of a classic symphony.

'Poor Platon!' she thought more than once; 'I have certainly been the most expensive whim that he has ever had; and he has never got the slightest entertainment out of me. I am very disagreeable to him; I have always been disagreeable to him. I was so at first because I could not help it, and I am so now because I like to be so. But I grant that it has never been quite fair to him. He might just as well have been all alone to amuse himself with his dancers, and comic singers, and people; I have been a white elephant to him. Certainly he has a kind of triumph in possessing the white elephant; he likes to feel I am here; when they all look after me in the Bois, or at the Opéra, he likes to think I belong to him. As somebody said, when people admire what is ours, it is as if they admired us. I am very much to him what the *bleu ciel* Sèvres for which he gave ten thousand pounds must be to Lord Dudley. The Sèvres is of no earthly use to him, and he would scarcely dare to touch it, and he would certainly never eat his cutlet or have his venison served on it; but it is something that everybody envies him, that nobody else has. When Platon gives great dinners to sovereigns and all kinds of *gros bonnets*, and I am opposite to him, I am sure he has the sort of feeling that Lord Dudley has about that *bleu ciel* service. After all, that is something; though, as the service was incomplete in quantity, so I am incomplete in sentiment. And then, when I meet him driving Mdlle. Chose in the Champs Elysées, I seem as if I did not see him; and I never say a syllable of objection if there are a hundred paragraphs in the *petits journaux* about himself and any number of Mdlles. Chose. If I had ever liked him, I should be angry and make a fuss. After all, he ought to know that, if indifference be not flattery, it is peace.'

So she soothed her conscience, but not always successfully; she had occasionally a passing touch of self-reproach, when she remembered how very little she had given her husband in return for the magnificent fortune, the boundless admiration, and the perfect independence, which she owed to him. She had at the bottom of her heart, though stifled and indistinct, a more sensitive and a higher-toned honour than most women; that instinct of honour told her that she had been, at all times, unjust and ungrateful to a man whose good qualities she refused to see, and even did her best to destroy, because his relation to her irritated her taste and temper, and his ugliness and want of intelligence filled her with disdain.

'If I had a daughter,' she thought, in those moments of candour and compunction, 'I think I should say to her, "Commit any sin and incur any sorrow you like rather than make a marriage without sympathy; it is the one crime which society has agreed to applaud as an act of wisdom and of virtue; but it is a crime nevertheless. One is so young, one does not know; one listens to people who urge all the advantages of it, and when one does know it is too late." However,' she added in her own musings, 'I dare say, if I had daughters, when they were old enough, I should do just the same as everybody else does; I should want them to make a *beau mariage*, and I should tell them to do it. It is the world which makes one like that. At the fair of Novgorod I once saw a little Simbirsh peasant arrested for stealing a necklace of blue and yellow beads; she burst out sobbing, and said she would not have taken it, but all the girls of her village had all their big beads, and she had none! In the big world we do the same. We want the big beads because other people have theirs. It is paltry; but then society is paltry at its best. They say, when you have entered an opium house, you may have made all the resolutions you will against smoking, you cannot keep them, the atmosphere gains on you, you yield, and smoke, and sink, like all the rest. The world is an opium house.'

Nature had designed her for something better than the opium house. Her intellect, her courage, and her chastity were all of great and fine quality, like the burnished blade of a sword, that is at once delicate and strong. But the world had absorbed her, and left little scope to those higher and nobler instincts. She was in her habits and her tastes a mere *élégante*, indolent, hard to please, hypercritical, of languid constitution, of infinite egotism. Given the impetus, this languor could alter, as by magic, into ardour, force, and energy; but the motive power could rarely be found which could rouse her, and she remained for the most part of her time a mere *mondaine*, of exquisite taste, of irresistible seduction, but useless, idle, contemptuous, cynical, vaguely disappointed, though all were at her feet, wanting, petulantly, like Alexander, more worlds to conquer. Sometimes in the ennui of the whole thing, and her dissatisfaction in it, she was only restrained from absolute evil by the consciousness of its vulgarity, and her own aversion to those indulgences in which most find their strongest temptation, but in which she only saw a humiliating and a grotesque affinity to the brutes.

As at four years old she had shrugged her small shoulders, with a sigh, before the bonbon boxes—'J'en ai tant!'—so at four-and-twenty years old she was supercilious to the whole world because it had given her so much, and yet had nothing better than that to give. And incredulous that there was anywhere anything better, she lived in her calorifère-heated rooms, like an orchid in a hothouse, and amused herself as with a game by the desires, the pains, the reproaches, the solicitations, the jealousies, which fretted and fumed themselves in that arena of her salon, whilst she remained as tranquil, as pitiless, and as indifferent as fate.

No woman had the world more completely beneath her feet, yet she, like Othmar, was consumed by that eternal ennui which is the penalty of those who possess too much, have seen and heard too much too early, and have been from childhood the objects of adulation and of speculation;—of all those, indeed, who have mind and heart enough not to find all their interests in society, and yet have not that poetic temper which would give them a sure consolation and a safe refuge in the uncloying loveliness of nature.

Ennui is unjustly looked upon as the characteristic of the frivolous type of humanity; on the contrary, the frivolous character is perfectly content with frivolity, and never tires of it. Ennui is rather the mark of those whose taste is too fine and whose instincts are too high to let them be satisfied with the excitement of, and the victories of, society, and yet who have too little of that simplicity, or of that impersonality, which makes the artistic temperament capable of entirely withdrawing from the world and living its own life, self-sustained.

This delicate patrician had the seed in her of great *roués*, of dauntless conspirators, of haughty territorial tyrants, of men and of women who had emptied thrones and filled them, and given law for life and death to multitudes of vassals; she could not be altogether content with the rosewater politics of modern drawing-rooms, with the harmless rivalry of toilettes and equipages, with the trivial pastimes and as trivial passions of society. She was a woman of the world to the tips of her fingers, yet she could not be altogether content with an existence of Courts, *chiffons*, flirtations, endless entertainments, and unlimited expenditure.

'They find us eccentric, capricious, autocratic, us Russians,' she said one day. 'I dare say we are so; they forget that, not a century ago, our great-grandparents were slaying Paul and Peter in their palaces, and could knout to death whole villages of men, women, and children, at their mere freak and fancy. I think it is very creditable to us not to be a thousand times worse than we are; our blood is made up of arack and of ice; we are the rude pines of the north French-polished!'

It was three o'clock in the day; she had given orders to be undisturbed. She had slept admirably for eight hours without any morphine. She had bathed twice, on her arrival and on her awaking, in warm water, opaque with otto of rose; she had breakfasted off her usual cup of cream and rolls made of milk. She was in a dreamy, drowsy, amused state of thought; and, as she lay on her couch in the boudoir, which was placed between her library and her dressing-chamber, her thoughts drifted persistently to the meeting of the dawn.

She felt very like Fate now, as she thought how odd it was that the first person she had met in Paris had been Othmar.

'He is very much changed for so short a time. He is not a whit more content,' she reflected, with pleasure.

The little room was the prettiest thing in all Paris. 'It is a casket for a pearl,' one of her adorers had said, and it seemed really a pity that for eight months out of the year the casket should be closed, and no ray of light ever enter it. Its furniture was of ivory, like that of the adjoining library, bed-room, and bathroom, and its hangings were of silvery satin embroidered with pale roses and apple-blossoms; Baudry had painted the ceiling with the story of Ædon and Procris: the glass in the windows was milk white, and the floor was covered with white bearskins: the atmosphere was like that of a hothouse, and as odorous; there were always a perfect seclusion and silence in it; the only sound which ever came there was the splash of a fountain in the garden below; it might have been set in the heart of the island of Alcina rather than in one of the great avenues of Paris. Here, lying back on one of her low couches with the air around her tropical, vaporous, dreamy, she mused within herself as to how she would deal with Othmar, a smile in her eyes and a doubt in her mind.

'Let him alone,' said her conscience.

'No,' said her vanity, and perhaps some other emotion also.

'He never harmed you; he only loved you, and obeyed you, and went away,' her conscience urged on her. But her vanity replied: 'That was the worst offence. There are commands which are most honoured by disobedience. There are wounds which ought to be cherished, not healed.'

Unless she chose that it should be otherwise, Othmar, she knew, would be a stranger to her all his life. They would meet, perhaps, in the world very often, but they would exchange commonplace courtesy, and remain as far asunder as two ships that pass each other on the same ocean course, unless she chose. Her better self said to her, 'Let him alone; he has tried to make another life for himself; he has failed, no doubt, but he has probably found a sort of peace, a kind of affection; if it can console him, do not disturb it.' But the habits of supremacy and of intrigue, the love of dominion, the intolerance of opposition, which were instinctive in her, and which all her many triumphs and her permitted egotism had fostered and confirmed, forbade her to resign herself to such passivity, and urged her to take up her empire over his life.

And she had a vague wish to see him there again beside her, a wish not very strong, but strong enough to move her. It was here, in this room, that he had first of all told her that he loved her, with words more daring and more imperious than any other had ventured to use in her presence; he was never like other people; he was probably no better, certainly no worse, than other men, but he was different: he pleased her imagination, he touched her sympathy; he was the only man with whom it had ever seemed to her that her life might have been lived harmoniously, with whom she might have understood something of that mystery of love in which she had never believed. To her temper it was the intrigue and intricacy of life which alone made it endurable, the unrolling of the ribbon of fate, the watching and controlling of the comedy of circumstances, which alone made it worth while to rise in the morning to the tedium of its routine.

'Is life worth living?' she said once, hearing of the title of a book of drawing-room philosophy. 'Yes, I think it is, if you are the cat, if you are the spider, if you are the eagle, if you are the dog; not if you are the mouse, or the fly, or the lamb, or the hare. Life is certainly worth living, too, if you regard it as what it is, a dramatic entertainment, diversion. This is the true use of riches, that it enables you to give yourself up to watching and controlling circumstances as if men and women were marionettes; it enables you to sit in your fauteuil and look on without moving unless you wish. I think that life must be always rather tiresome to anybody over ten years old, but the only possible way to endure it is to regard it as a spectacle, as a comedy, or, as Manteuffel has said, that a general sitting in his saddle regards the battlefield he governs.'

This was what she said and felt in her cynical moods, and she was cynical now on her return to Paris; she had left her better self behind her in the snow-drifts of her own country. The woman who had spoken so tenderly of Boganof scarcely existed in her; she lived in an atmosphere of adulation, excitation, ennui, and frivolous occupations. The heroic protectress of the Siberian exile had scarcely a trait in common with her; she spent half the day in the discussion of new costumes with her tailors, and the other half surrounded by flatterers and courtiers in the pursuit of new distractions.

Analysis was so natural to her that it seemed to her in no situation or even crisis of her life would she have abandoned it. There is a well-known physiologist, now head of a famous laboratory, who, when his son died, a boy of twelve, scarcely waited for the child's last breath to plunge his scalpel into the still warm body in hopes of some discovery of the law of life. If she had had any emotions she would have done a similar thing; she would have dissected them even if they had sprung from her own life blood.

CHAPTER XXXVII.

'Is Madame Napraxine a good woman?' said Yseulte timidly one day in her own drawing-room to Melville, whilst she coloured to the eyes as she pronounced the name.

'Good, my dear!' echoed Friederich Othmar, who overheard and replied to the question. 'The epithet is comically incongruous. She would be as horrified if she heard you as if you called her *ma bourgeoise*.'

Melville laughed a little despite himself, and hesitated before giving his own reply: he was embarrassed. How could he as a priest say to this innocent creature what he as a man of the world knew to be the truth; that the simple classifications of good and bad can no more suffice to describe the varieties of human character than the shepherd's simple names for herb and flower can suffice for the botanist's floral nomenclature and complicated subdivisions.

'She has very noble qualities,' he said at length. 'Perhaps they are somewhat obscured by the habits of the world. She is of an exceedingly complicated character. I fear I scarcely know her well enough to describe her with perfect correctness. But I know some noble acts of her life; one I may tell you.'

And he related to her the episode of Boganof.

Yseulte listened with wonder: to her youthful imagination her one enemy appeared in all the dark hues with which youth ever paints what it dislikes and dreads, exaggerated like the rainbow light with which it decks what it loves. All the highest instincts of her nature were touched to sympathy by what she now heard, but a pain of which Melville knew nothing contracted her heart as she thought that if her husband had indeed loved such a woman as this, it was natural that she would for ever retain her power on him.

'And she is so beautiful!' she added, with a little sigh. Melville looked at her in surprise.

'Who has been talking to her?' he wondered as he said aloud:

'There are women more beautiful. You have but to look in your mirror, my child. But she has a surpassing grace, an incomparable fascination, some of which springs, perhaps, from her very defects. She is a woman essentially of the modern type, all nerves and scepticism intermingled; ironical, incredulous, indifferent, yet capable of heroic *coups de tête*; dissatisfied with the worldly life and yet incapable of living any other; the Réné of Chateaubriand, made female and left without a God.'

'Except her tailor!' said Friederich Othmar, who approached the little nook in which Melville was seated in the boudoir.

'Pardon me,' said Melville, with a smile. 'Madame Napraxine's tailor is but her slave, like every one else whom she employs or encounters. The king of *couturiers* trembles before her, he is so afraid of her displeasure; if she blame his creations they are ruined. She makes *la pluie et le beau temps* in the world of fashion.'

'And yet she could do what you say for that unhappy man in Siberia?' murmured Yseulte, who had listened with seriousness and some perplexity to all that had been said of one in whom her instinct felt was the enemy of her life.

'You should understand a character which is made up of contradictions, my dear,' interrupted the Baron; 'for you have one beside you every day in Otho's. Your own is formed with just a few broad, simple, fair lines, ruled very straight on the old pattern, which was in use before the Revolution, or even farther back than that, in the days of Anne of Bretagne and of Blanche of Castille. But your husband's—and some other people's—is a tangled mass of unformed desires and of widely-opposed qualities which are for ever in conflict, and are as unsatisfactory and as indefinite as any *impressionniste's* picture.'

Yseulte did not hear; she was absorbed in her own reflections; her face was very grave.

'M. le Baron, you cannot have everything,' said Melville, gaily. 'Your age has destroyed the *femme croyante*. Nature, which always avenges herself, gives you the *femme du monde*, which, in its lowest stages, becomes the *cabotine*, and in its highest just such an ethereal, capricious, tantalising combination of the finest culture and the most languid scepticism, as captivates and tortures her world in the person of the Princess Napraxine.'

'Excuse me in my turn if I say that you are quite mistaken,' said Friederich Othmar. 'The two species of womankind have existed since the days of Athens and of Rome, and modern theology and modern scepticism have nothing to do with either of them. Penelope and Circe are as old as the islands and the seas. If you will not find me impertinent, I cannot help saying that ecclesiastics always remind me of the old story (I think it is in Moore's Diary) of the grazier's son who went to Switzerland, and was only impressed by one fact—that bullocks were very cheap there. Christianity is a purely modern thing. What are eighteen centuries in the history of the world? Yet every churchman refers every virtue and every vice of human nature to the influence or the absence of this purely modern creed, which has, after all, not one tenth of the magnetic power of absorption of Buddhism and nothing like the grasp on the mind of a multitude which Islamism has possessed.'

Friederich Othmar had always an especial pleasure in teazing Melville, and in contemplating the address with which the trained talent of the theologian vaulted over the difficulties which his reason was forced to acknowledge.

As Melville was about to reply, the groom of the chambers entered and announced 'Madame la Princesse Napraxine.'

Yseulte rose with a startled look upon her young face, which was not yet trained to conceal what she felt beneath that mask of serenity and smiling indifference which makes the most impenetrable of all masks. Her cheeks flushed, her eyes had a momentary look of bewilderment. She did not hear the words of graceful greeting with which her visitor answered the courtesy she mechanically made.

Melville, who himself felt a little guilty, hastened to her rescue, and the Baron, as he rolled a low chair for the newcomer, thought to himself, 'What a pity Otho is not here; it is always better to have those situations gone through, and over. The poor child!—so happy as she has been! It will be a pity if Circe come. But Circe always comes. How can Melville pretend that Circe is anything new, or has only sprung into existence because women do not go to church! Madame Napraxine is precisely the same kind of *charmeresse* that Propertius used to write odes to on his tablets; the type was more consistent then, because in our days costume is incongruous, and life is more complicated, and people are more tired, but it remains integrally the same.'

Nadine Napraxine meanwhile was saying:

'Your people were unwilling to let me in because it was not your day; but I insisted. When one desires a thing very much one always insists till one gets it. I find Paris talking of nothing but the Countess Othmar; I was eager to claim from her the privilege of an old friend.'

It was said with sweetness, apparent frankness, and all her own inimitable grace. She lightly touched, with the softest, slightest kiss, the cheeks of Yseulte, which grew warm and then cold. Not appearing to notice her embarrassment, Nadine Napraxine continued to string her pretty, careless, courteous phrases together with that tact which is the most useful and the most graceful of all the talents. Yseulte had all a girl's embarrassment before her, and that dignity which was an instinct in her became, by contrast, almost stiffness.

'Someone has told her of me,' thought Nadine, with amusement and irritation combined. It at once offended her and pleased her that she should be a source of pain to this girl—to how many women had she been so, and without mercy! Well, why would they not learn to keep to themselves the wandering thoughts of their lovers and their lords? 'This child is beautiful,' she said to herself with candour; 'how can she fail with him. No doubt she loves him herself; men are not thankful. *Tenez la dragée haute* is the only motto for their subjection.'

She studied Yseulte with attention and interest, and without malice. She frankly admired this beauty so different to her own; this union of high-bred stateliness and childish naïveté which seemed to her just such a manner as some young châtelaine of some old Breton or Norman tower would have had in the days of the Reine Isabeau; she did full justice to it. The irritation she had felt when she had walked in the moonlight through the grass lands at Zaraïzoff, and thought of the château of Amyôt, had ceased the moment that she had entered the atmosphere of Paris. Othmar had believed that he had been cold as marble in that momentary meeting, but she had seen in it that her power over him was undiminished. She knew very well that soon or late he who had defied her would be once more as a reed in her hands. She was in no haste to try her force; she could rely on it in the calmness of certainty. She was very amiable to his wife; but she had a little touch of good-natured condescension in her amiability which made the pride of the girl shrink as under an affront which could not be resented; the very young always suffer under a kindness which tacitly reminds them, by its unspoken superiority, of their own inexperience and their own defects. The ironical smile, the slight suggestive phrases, the very indulgence, as to a child, of Nadine Napraxine were as so many thorns in the heart of Yseulte, who had none of that vanity which might have rendered her indifferent to them.

It was not so much an emotion, but a certain sentiment—half interest, half irritation—which brought her to the great house of which, in a moment of impulse, he had made this child mistress. 'They try to give it a false air of home,' she thought, with her merciless accuracy of penetration, 'but they do not succeed. It is always a barn—a barn gilded and painted like Versailles: but a barn. Perhaps they succeed better at Amyôt, and perhaps they do not. He always hated this huge house, and he was very right in his taste. It is made to entertain in, not to be happy in. If he were happy he would go far away to that castle by the blue Adrian Sea that I saw within a few leagues of Miramar.'

With that thought she had gone through the succession of great rooms, grand and uninteresting as the rooms of the Escurial, until she had reached one of the drawing-rooms, with its painted panels of children romping in orchards and gardens, and there had found Yseulte sitting at her tapestry like some young dame of the time of Bayard or the Béarnais, a large hound at her feet, the two old men beside her.

'What colouring! She is like a pastel of Emile Lévy's!' she had thought, with an appreciation which was entirely sincere, as she kissed the girl's reluctant, roseleaf-like cheek: she really felt not the slightest ill-will towards her; on the contrary, she was moved to a compassion, none the less genuine that it was based on something very like disdain; the disdain of the wise for the simple, of the certainly victorious for the predestined vanquished, of the snake-charmer for those who let the snake kill them.

With her most charming grace, with that seduction which made it impossible for anyone in her presence to be her enemy, she renewed her acquaintance with the wife of Othmar, speaking pretty and gracious words of recognition and of admiration. Yseulte preserved a self-control admirable for one so young, to whom the necessities for such reserve were a new and painful lesson; but she was unable to keep the change of colour in her cheeks, and the expression in her candid eyes betrayed her to the quick perception of her guest.

'You have come to honour Paris, Princess?' said the Baron, to cover the embarrassment and the constraint of Yseulte.

'One always comes to Paris, Baron,' answered Nadine Napraxine, raising her eyeglass and gazing at the girl through it, with all the cruel, careless scrutiny of a woman of the world; her luminous eyes wanted no assistance of the sort, but it was a weapon—unkind as a dagger on occasion. 'One always comes to Paris. It is the toy-shop where we dolls of the world get mended when we are battered and bruised. We come for our hair, for our teeth, for our complexions; at any rate, for our gowns; and then when we arrive we remain. The Republic may push its iron roller, as Berlioz says it does, over the world; it rolls on wheels of lead; but it cannot prevent Paris from being always an empire, and always the *urbs* for us. I do not love Paris as passionately as most Russians do, yet even I admit that there is no other city where one finds so little monotony. Even in Paris, alas! as Marivaux said long ago, everybody has two eyes, one nose, and one mouth, and one sighs in vain for a little variety of outline.'

'If I remember,' said the Baron, 'Marivaux was more merciful to humanity than is Madame Napraxine; he admitted that even with such homely materials as two eyes, a nose, and a mouth, one could obtain infinite variety in expression; no two physiognomies are alike.'

'Perhaps in Marivaux's time men did not imitate the *chic anglais*!' said Nadine Napraxine. 'I see very little variety myself. Everybody is terribly like everyone else, except the Comtesse Othmar,' she added, with her charming smile, 'who is only like Hope nursing Love, or some other picture of a fairer day than ours.'

Yseulte, pained at herself for her want of self-command, coloured hotly under the compliment, in which her alarmed sensitiveness fancied there was hidden a sarcasm. She did not know of what picture Nadine Napraxine spoke, and she thought—'Does she mean that Hope was barren and foolish, that Love did not care?' She remembered the silver amorino and the empty gourd.

Directly appealed to, a moment later, she murmured something at random; she did not well know what; she grew first pale, then red; she seemed constrained and stupid, void of ideas, and stiff in manner. Friederich Othmar could have broken his cane about her shoulders in his vexation.

'Heavens and earth!' he thought, 'if you let yourself be magnetised at the first sight of an imagined rival, what will you do before the reality when you meet it? My poor little girl! It is not the women who adore a man, and are struck dumb because they see another woman whom he has once loved, who obtain any influence over him, or possess any charm whatever for him. Who is to tell you that? who is to open your eyes and harden your heart? who is to make you understand that you are as lovely as the morning, but that if you do not acquire self-control, wit, indifference, all the armoury of the world's weapons, she will pass over you as artillery sweeps over the daisy in the grass.'

But he could not say his impatient thoughts aloud; he could not even, by his own readiness of language and easy persiflage, contrive wholly to hide the uneasiness and restraint which the presence of her guest brought upon Yseulte, and which she herself was at once too young and too frank to dissemble. They amused the Princess Napraxine, and they gratified her infinitely. She had not the slightest pity for them; she had never suffered from any such awkwardness herself.

'You are cruel, Princess,' Melville ventured to murmur as he rose and bade her adieu.

'Have you only now discovered that?' said Nadine. 'And I do not know why you should discover it especially now, or why, even if it were truth, you should be in any way astonished. Thirty years of the confessional should have taught you that women are always cruel. Are you never cruel?' she said aloud, turning to Yseulte. 'Ah, then, your dog will disobey you and your horse run away with you, my dear Countess!'

'Is there no power in affection?' said Yseulte bravely, feeling her colour come and go, and conscious that she had made an absurd reply.

Madame Napraxine smiled with a little look of indulgent amusement, which made the girl thrill to the tips of her fingers.

'You are still in the age of illusions, my love. I dare say you even write poetry. Do you not write poetry? I am sure you must have a little velvet book and a silver pencil somewhere. It is so delightful to see anyone so young,' she added, with seriousness, to Friederich Othmar. 'The children are not young now, are never young. I do not think I ever was; I have no recollection of it. If I had daughters, I would send them to those Dames de Sainte Anne—away in Brittany, is it not?—if it be they who have made your nephew's wife what she is. I did not believe there was any place left, simple enough and sweet and solemn enough to make a girlhood like a garden lily. Othmar has been very happy to have gathered the lily.'

There were both reality and admiration in many of her words, but the last phrase was not so sincere. Yseulte, overhearing, thought, with a pang, 'She knows that he is not happy!' Her heart swelled. She felt that this exquisite woman, so little her senior in actual years, so immeasurably her superior in knowledge, tact, and power, laughed at her even as she praised her. 'How could she know that I wrote poetry?' thought the child, conscious of many a poor little verse, the unseen, carefully-hidden, timid offspring of a heart too full, written with a pencil in the leafy recesses of the woods of Amyôt, in that instinctive longing for adequate expression which is born of a great love. The chance phrase gave Nadine Napraxine in her sight all the irresistible fascination of a magician. She felt as if those languid, luminous eyes could read all the secrets of her soul—secrets so innocent, all pregnant with the memory of Othmar—secrets pure, wholesome, and harmless as the violets that the mosses hid in the Valois woods of Amyôt.

'Well, what do you think of her?' asked Friederich Othmar when she had left the house. Yseulte hesitated.

'I can believe that she has a great charm,' she answered with some effort. 'She has a fascination that one feels whether one will or no——'

She paused and unconsciously sighed.

'She is the greatest *charmeresse* in Europe,' replied Friederich Othmar. 'No other words describe her. She is not a Cleopatra or a Mary Stuart. She would never have had an Actium or a Kirk's Field. She would never have so blundered. She has no passions; she would be a better woman if she had. She is entirely chaste only because she is absolutely indifferent. It creates her immense power over men. She remains ice while she casts them into hell.' He stopped abruptly, remembering to whom he spoke, and added, 'Her visit was a most rare honour to you, my dear; she seldom deigns to go in person anywhere; her servants leave her cards, and the fortunate great ladies who are the recipients of them may go and see her on her day, and take their chance of receiving a few words from her. She is one of those exceptional women who have no intimate friends of their own sex, or hardly any; men——'

He paused, asked leave to light a cigarette, and walked with it awhile about the room. Yseulte did not take up his unfinished phrase by an interrogation.

'Have you no inquisitiveness?' thought Friederich Othmar. She was, indeed, full of restless and painful curiosity concerning the woman who had just left her presence, but she would not allow herself to utter a word of it. She thought it would be disloyalty to her husband.

Some fifteen minutes later Othmar himself entered.

'Madame Napraxine has just honoured us *in propriâ personâ*,' said the Baron, looking at him with intention.

'Indeed!' said Othmar. 'It was most amiable of her,' he added, after a moment's pause; but to the penetration or to the imagination of his uncle it seemed that he spoke with embarrassment and annoyance. Yseulte had resumed her work at her tapestry. The cruel sense that she was not wanted there, that she had been brought there only out of pity, as a kind hand gives a stray animal a home, weighed on her more and more. She did not see all that others saw in her; all the attraction of her youth, and her innocence and her beauty. She had too sincere a humility for any idea of her own charms to console her. She was wise enough to perceive that the world flattered her because she was a rich man's wife, but in her own eyes she remained the same that she had been under the grey shadows of Faïel.

'If I were only myself again to-morrow, they would never think of me,' she said to herself, with a wisdom born out of the poverty and obscurity in which her childish years had been spent. She was passionately grateful to Othmar, as well as devoted to him; but the suggestion that she was in no way necessary to his happiness, was even a burden and a constraint to him, had been harshly set before her by the words of Blanchette, and it was corroborated by a thousand trifles of look, and speech, and accident. His very entrance into her room had nothing of the warmth of a man who returns to what he loves; he came there so evidently because he felt that courtesy and custom required it of him.

The Baron understood what was passing in her thoughts as she bent her fair head over her tapestry-frame, the severity of her black velvet gown serving to enhance, by its contrast, the whiteness of her throat, the youthfulness of her features, the suppleness and vigour of her form. He longed to say to her, 'My child, do not fret because he is no longer your lover—is even, perhaps, that of some one else; it is always so in marriage, even in love. There is always one who cares long, and one who cares little. It will not matter to you in the end; you will learn to lead your own life; you will have your children. I do not think you will have your lovers, as most of them do, but you will get reconciled to accepting life on a lower plane than your youthful imagination placed it on at first.'

He would have liked to say that, and much more, to her, but he did not venture. She made no confidence, no appeal for sympathy; and after all, for aught he knew, she might be entirely content with her husband's ardour, or his lack of it. She was but a child still, and had little knowledge of the passions of men.

Othmar did not say that he had met his wife's guest as she left his house.

She had given him her prettiest smile.

'The Countess Othmar is quite lovely; and what a perfect manner!' she had said. 'What does she say to all your pessimism, to all your *boutades*? Does she understand them? You must send her to hear a course of Caro. Her mind can hardly be metaphysical yet. She is at the age to eat bonbons and expect caresses.'

Then she had made him a little careless sign of farewell, and her black horses had borne her through the great gates of gilded bronze of the house which always seemed to him oppressive as a gaol. The words were harmless, playful, amiable; yet they had annoyed him. He understood that she ridiculed his marriage, and that she divined that it had but little place in his affections, and as little hold upon his thoughts.

'Poor child!' he had said involuntarily, as he mounted his staircase to enter the presence of Yseulte.

CHAPTER XXXVIII.

When Nadine Napraxine came into her boudoir on New Year's day, she smiled a little to see it blocked with flowers. She had always discountenanced any other gifts than flowers. Whoever had presumed to offer her anything else would have run the risk of having his name struck off her list of acquaintances.

'All those *gros cadeaux* are so vulgar,' she was wont to say. 'A branch of lilac—a tea-rose—nothing else. No; you must not send the lilac in a *cloisonné* Limoges vase, or the roses in a *repoussé* silver bowl; I should send you your vase or your bowl back to you; you have no kind of right to suppose that I want vases or bowls; but just the branch, just the rose, you may send if you like.'

They trembled, and dared not disobey; the lilacs or the roses came by the scores, with the greatest names of Europe attached to them; and her courtiers managed ingeniously to spend many thousands of francs by means of the rarest of the orchids, fulfilling her commands in the letter, though breaking them in the spirit.

She smiled now as she came into her favourite room this morning, when fog and frost together reigned without. All the orchid world was there to welcome her, brilliant and ethereal as the hues of sunrise.

'They love to be extravagant,' she thought, with a little contempt. 'If one limit them to flowers they manage to spend as much as if they bought jewels. It is very vulgar, all that sort of thing. If I cared for any one of them, I think I should like him to bring me a little bunch of corn-cockles—just by way of change.'

She glanced here and there at a name, but, for the most part, did not even trouble herself to look who was the sender of this or of that.

'*C'est toute la bande!*' she murmured, with an impatient amusement, knowing that every man in Paris, with rank sufficient to be able to dare to do so, had sent his floral tribute there.

She rang for her favourite servant Paul; when he appeared she said to him, 'Take all those cards off those baskets and bouquets; they look as if they were ticketed for a horticultural show.' So Paul, obedient, swept away the visiting cards with his swift and silent touch, and the senders of them were not even honoured by her caring to know their names; their gifts were all blended in one mass of blossom as indifferent to her as themselves.

Paul, as he retired with the cards crushed in his hand, thought to himself with grim amusement, 'If only those *beaux messieurs* would understand that Nadège Fedorowna cares no more for any one of them than she will care for those flowers when they are yellow and withered to-morrow.'

'If somebody would bring me the corn-cockles!' she herself thought, with a little laugh.

At that moment there came a timid tap on the door which separated her boudoir from the great salons. She recognised it with a little shiver, such as a nervous woman will give when she sees an unpleasant or uncouth animal; only she was not nervous herself; she was merely impressionable and irritated.

'Come in,' she said impatiently.

The door opened behind the satin hangings, and Platon Napraxine entered.

'How many times must I request you to pay me the common respect of sending to know if I be visible?' she said, with that hauteur which he dreaded, as a prisoner in the fortress of Peter and Paul dreads the sight of the knout.

'I beg your pardon,' he murmured humbly. 'It is not our day, but I thought you would allow me to take advantage of the French New Year to—to—to bring you a little gift. Do not be angry, Nadine——'

He spoke very submissively and with a timidity which made his high-coloured cheeks grow paler. He had for many a year abandoned all hope of being any nearer to the woman who was his wife than the marble of the steps which she descended to her carriage; yet he could not help having, every now and then, a foolish impulse to approach her in affection, a wistful fancy that perhaps—perhaps—at last——

He laid on her knee as he spoke a velvet case, with her crown and initials in gold upon it.

'My dear Platon, what nonsense!' she said, with some real annoyance, and she murmured to herself: 'In half an hour he will take something similar to half a dozen *cocottes*!'

But she could do no less than open the case, which was filled by a necklace, earrings, and a small crown for the hair in pink pearls.

Platon Napraxine watched her wistfully as she looked at them with a listless indifference. If he could only please her once! If he could only once see that beautiful contemptuous mouth smile kindly on him.

'There is not one of them worth her little finger,' he thought, meaning the companions and consolers of his life.

'I think you have no pink pearls; it is the only thing you have not,' he said; as humble still as a chidden dog. 'Will you not let me wish you *bonne fête*, Nadine? I——'

He took her hand and carried it to his lips. She drew it away, not angrily, but with a profound indifference.

'I cannot see why one day in the year is any more than another, that we should make speeches upon it,' she said, shutting up the jewel case. 'The pearls are quite charming. It is too good of you. Only, you know I do not in the least see why you should give me things; I really do not want them——'

It was the *'j'en ai tant'* of her five-year-old philosophy.

'I know you do not want them,' said her husband with a blank sense of foolish disappointment, foolish because his hope had been foolish. 'But still most women never have jewels enough. I do not mean that I ever thought you would care for them, but still it is the custom—and—one never likes the day to go by,—if you would say a kind word——'

'My dear Platon,' she said wearily, yet with a certain amusement at his stupidity, 'why will you persist in that superstition that one day is any more than all the others?—and not even a Russian day either! You, who are such a Slavophil, should have ignored a French New Year's day as quite pagan and indecent. The pearls are very pretty; I will put them on to-night, if that will please you. Only—only—you know I am not very fond of that sort of presents. Are you sure you have not another similar case in your pocket that you are going to take this morning to that very handsome new house in the Avenue Villiers? All the houses are new there, but that is newest——'

Napraxine coloured dully with a dual sense of embarrassment and ridicule.

He was silent.

'Are you sure?' said his wife, with her head leaning back on her cushions and her demure smile gleaming beneath the lashes of her half-closed eyelids.

'Nadine!' stammered Napraxine, in mingled discomfiture and eagerness, which made him blunder more and more. 'What can one do when you—you,—as God is above us, if you had not turned me adrift years ago as if I were a monster, I would never have looked at another woman. You do not believe it, but I would not. Even now, I would leave them all if you said a word,—if—if——'

She rose and laid the case of pearls down on a table near her.

'My dear Prince,' she said in her iciest tones, though, in her own heart, she could very willingly have laughed aloud, 'I see you have indeed mistaken your road to the Avenue de Villiers. Do you think you can purchase my—kindness—as you do that of your mistresses? Pray let this be the last of such blunders. You have not been guilty of them for many years. Do not begin now. They offend me. You will only ruffle, very disagreeably and uselessly, the amiable understanding on which we have agreed to live.'

'When did I ever agree?'

His face was darkly flushed, his voice was husky and had a tremor in it, something savage and imperious began to wake in him and tell him that after all this delicate and disdainful woman was his;—but her languid lids opened wholly, and her calm, luminous eyes looked him full in the face with that look with which the keeper can daunt, by sheer power of will, the animal which could trample him into dust and tear him into atoms.

'Pray, do not let us re-open a discussion which has been closed for six years,' she said in her softest, coldest voice. 'I am quite sure you meant well; I never bear malice; I will wear your pearls to-night. We have a dinner, I think; for d'Aumale, is it not? *Bonne fête, mon ami.* Think what a troubled life you would have if I cared about that new house, and be grateful. Please send Paul here. He must take away some of this lilac. So much of it will give me *migraine*.'

Napraxine stifled as best he could some oath which he dared not utter aloud, and went slowly and sullenly out of her presence, sensible of an ignominious dismissal. His glance as he went dwelt with suspicion on the baskets and bouquets which made the room and the adjoining rooms gardens of orchids and odontoglossum, of gardenias and of tea-roses.

'Is there one among them,' he thought, 'for whom she cares?'

He was nothing to her: but he would be something to such an one if ever he could find his foe.

He was hurt, wounded, humiliated, infuriated, all in one; conscious of a defeat which made him grotesque in her sight, sensible of an act of unwisdom and of sentimentality which had only placed him lower than ever in the estimation of a woman whom he was furiously conscious that he still loved and still desired.

When the hangings of the door had closed behind him, his wife laughed with an amusement which her sense of courtesy had controlled before, and put a tea-rose in the bosom of her gown.

'How stupid, how intensely stupid, to come to me as he goes to his *cocottes*,' she thought, with that irritation and ennui which were the only emotions which he ever aroused in her. 'And to renew that sort of argument as if we were two greengrocers living at Montmartre! Decidedly, when the *bon Dieu* made poor Platon, he left out of his composition every vestige of tact; and really tact is the only quality that it is absolutely necessary for everybody to have to prevent them from irritating others. Who could have imagined that after six years he would begin again like that!—he has always a little access of tenderness at the end of the year; last time he gave me a dreadful Chinese idol as big as himself with green eyes; some dealer had told him it was very precious: he did not know, he never knows; I wonder if there were anybody so stupid in all the world; I am only astonished that he did not send for Sachs and Mitz as an agreeable surprise for me!'

'Yes, Paul,' she said aloud, 'take away most of those flowers, they make my head ache; and give that case to Jeanne to put up in the jewel-safe. Tell Fedor that I shall want the horses in an hour.'

'How very stupid some women must be,' she reflected often, 'to let themselves be dictated to, and denied, and bullied, and worried by their husbands. Nothing is so easy to manage as a man, if you only begin in the right way with him. All depends on how you begin; it is just like a horse; if you do not make him feel that you are his superior at once, he will take advantage of you for ever. I remember my mother saying to me before my marriage: "Ménage ton mari, sois bien douce." Now, if I had listened to her, I should have had Platon on my shoulders all my life; I dare say, even, he would have expected me to please him, and to listen to him, and to accept all his absurdities. But I froze him from the first; he has always been intensely afraid of me. Of two people there is always one who is afraid, and I preferred that it should be he. It just shows what mind can do over matter.'

She looked listlessly at a pile of telegrams which her servant had brought in with him and laid on the little table near her.

'They will all say the same thing,' she thought indifferently, as she opened two or three which contained the usual greetings of the New Year from her innumerable relatives and friends in other countries and at other courts; no Russian, of course, amongst them.

'If people must have it that a year begins, which is utterly absurd, why did they not take pretty pink and white April instead of this ugly, shivering, frost-bitten January?' she said to her dog Dauphin, as she glanced through the tedious compliments of the telegrams. At last, amidst them, there was one which made her change colour as she read it. It was from Lady Brancepeth, away on her estates in the north of England. It was only a line; it said:

'My brother has been killed on the ice in the Gulf of S. Lawrence.'

There were no details, only the bare fact, as it had been brought with the same crushing curtness by the electric cable from the western to the eastern shores of the Atlantic.

Nadine Napraxine read it three times without at the first realising or believing it. The news gave her a shock; not a great one, but still a kind of chilly pain and vague terror. A mist swam for a moment before her eyes; a sorrow, which was quite sincere, moved her as the sense of what she read gradually grew more and more distinct. A sudden remembrance smote her of Geraldine, as she had seen him first some three years earlier, standing on the beach at Biarritz, clad in his blue sea-clothes, with the sun shining full on his fair frank features and in his clear, happy, candid eyes. He had looked at her; his sister had beckoned to him, and had said carelessly: 'Ralph, is it possible that you do not know Madame Napraxine?' and he had come up to them over the rough red rocks, the sun and the wind playing in his bright hair. And then, life had never again been quite the same to him, and now it was over for ever. He was dead, just thirty years old!

'Pauvre garçon!' she said, with genuine regret, as she had said the same words when they had told her that the young Louis Napoléon had been killed at Isandula. It was not the regret for which the dead man, thinking of her as the frozen night had closed in on him and over the wastes of ice-bound waters, perchance had hoped. 'Pauvre garçon!' she murmured where she sat, amidst the profusion of the flowers. For the moment she felt cold in her room, which was as warm as a summer day, and through whose double windows of opalescent glass no breath of the outer air could penetrate.

'I suppose they will say I did this too!' she thought with impatience, her memory reverting to the death of young Seliedoff even whilst she said again very softly to herself, 'Pauvre garçon!'

She was sincerely sorry; she felt nothing of that more passionate and personal pain which once Geraldine might not unnaturally have hoped that his death would excite in her, but a sincere regret mingled with a kind of annoyance that men who had loved her would always go and run some tragic risks, so that they perished miserably:—and then the world blamed her.

'I, who detest tragedies!' she said to the little dog. 'When the majority of men, too, always live too long, live to have gout, and use spectacles, and grow tiresome!'

'Pauvre garçon, pauvre garçon!' she murmured once more, in the only threnody which occurred to her: how could he go and get drowned in the S. Lawrence, where the ice was surely as thick as in the Neva? She had always liked to play at being Providence to her world, a very capricious and unkind Providence indeed, but still one which decided their destinies without any reference to their desires as Providence is always permitted to do. She did not like these rude gusts of uncalled for accident which blew out the lives which she held in her hand as if they were so many tapers!

'Pauvre garçon!'

He had grown very wearisome, he had been even disposed to become exacting, he had wearied her, and she had not known very well how to get rid of him; but still it was a pity. He had had a great position, he was an only son, his own people were very fond of him, he was better than most of the men of his age and rank; she had for once the sensation that one feels when one has broken a rare piece of china,—the sensation of having done a silly thing, an irreparable thing.

'I never told him to go to Canada!' she said to herself. No: she had only told him that he wearied her. So he had wearied her; he had never been too amusing at the best of times. It was not her fault that he had become tiresome; they all became so; they had no originality. Still it was a pity; she saw his fair frank face, with its eyes so blue and so wistful, looking at her as he had stood to hear his sentence that last day we saw La Jacquemerille.

'I do not think I said anything unkind to him that day,' she reflected; and then the little smile that was so often on her lips came on them a moment as she thought: 'To be sure, I told him to marry somebody—anybody.'

Well, he was dead, and before he was thirty; with all his courage and gallantry and wealth, and the many people who loved him at home all powerless to save him from the black chasm of the yawning ice; and she was not so very sorry after all; she honestly wished she could feel more sorrow. She had never known real sorrow but once, when her father had been found dead in his writing-room in the Embassy at Vienna.

'Platon will be more sorry,' she thought, 'he always likes his worst enemies so much!'

Then she rang again for Paul, and told him to take the telegram to the Prince if he was still in the house.

Napraxine, in five minutes' time, not venturing to return in person, wrote to her on the back of the printed message:

'I am grieved indeed. Would you desire to postpone the dinner of to-night?'

She wrote back to him:

'That would be too infinitely ridiculous; though it is certainly a great pity, he was no relation of ours, only a *bonne connaissance*!'

'A *bonne connaissance*!' exclaimed Napraxine when he read the pencilled words. That was all the requiem given to the drowned man, whose battered and disfigured body was then on its way homeward, on the deck of a vessel which was ploughing a stormy way through dusky mountainous Atlantic waves!

She sat still a little while, looking through the remaining telegrams and casting them aside; all the rest were the mere congratulations of the season.

'I wonder when people will invent anything new!' she thought as she threw the last aside. 'To think that the Romans five and twenty centuries ago were also running about and visiting and sending cakes and taking flowers, because what they called a new year had come! I suppose the world will never liberate itself from the *camisole de force* of idiotic customs.'

She wrote a telegram of sympathy to the sister of Geraldine as she had written a letter of condolence to the mother of Seliedoff; then she had herself wrapped in sealskin from head to foot and prepared for her drive in the Bois.

'When I am gone, open the windows, Paul,' she said to the servant, who was so astonished that he ventured to ask if he heard aright, knowing that his lady loved warm air as a palm does.

'Open the windows and leave them open,' she repeated. She looked at all the hot-house blossoms and thought, with that cruelty which was latent in her side by side with her higher qualities, 'They will all be withered in an hour. Paul will tell all the valets, they will tell all their masters——'

The fancy diverted her. She liked flowers, but she liked a little cruelty like this much better. It would be wholesome for all those men to know how she valued their New Year's gifts.

'Women nowadays make them so vain,' she said to herself. 'If it were not for me, they would never get a lesson at all.'

To some the lesson had been severe, severe as the severity of death; but that fact scarcely affected her conscience.

She did not stop her carriage to speak to any of her acquaintances, for she supposed that the news of Geraldine's death would by this time be known in Paris, where he had so many friends, and knew that everyone would take pleasure in saying to her—'Mais comment donc? Est-ce bien vrai?—' It would be so tiresome!

'I cannot help it if they kill themselves!' she said to herself as her horses sped along the frosty roads. 'Society will blame me now, but I imagine they would have blamed me much more if I had gone away into his north-country mists with poor Geraldine as he would have liked me to do; he was so sensational, poor fellow, and so romantic under his English awkwardness. Englishmen are like that; they can seldom say anything they mean properly, but they are very romantic under it all; they are always ready to compromise themselves, despite their decorum, and they have just the dogged fidelity of their own bulldogs.'

He had been better than most of them certainly.

She felt a certain pain as she went through the chill sharp air and heavy mists, and remembered how many times she had seen Geraldine come riding through the trees, and how boyishly his face had flushed whenever he had seen her first! Poor foolish fellow! to leave all his possessions and interests and duties, and to go out to Ottawa, where he had no earthly business to be, as if going to Ottawa were likely to deliver him of her memory! That was so truly an Englishman's idea, to change latitude and longitude and think you left behind you any inconvenient passion you might be haunted with by merely changing your climate and your food! 'Poor Ralph! Poor Ralph! I think there was nothing on earth tragic, ridiculous, or abominable that he would not have done if I had ordered him to do it—except that he would never have killed Platon. I do not think even I could have made him kill Platon. That is the sort of scruple an Englishman always has, alone of all men in the world.'

'I suppose she knows it, but she does not care,' said many persons, looking after her as their wont was, as she flashed past them, nothing scarcely seen of her except her luminous eyes looking out from the brown lustre of the sealskins, whilst she made an almost imperceptible gesture of her head to the innumerable salutations that marked her course.

'When we get rid of the *camisole de force*,' she said to herself, 'we shall get rid of bowing to each other; it is insane, when everyone meets everyone else morning, noon, and night, to be obliged to jerk one's head fifty times every quarter of an hour when one is out of doors!'

She scarcely moved hers, indeed, but still it was a trouble; it was to avoid the trouble that she sometimes took those long solitary drives into the open country, of which the motive constantly perplexed her world. To any other woman they would have attributed assignations, but no one could ever do that to the Princess Napraxine; her absolute indifference was too notorious a fact, and the dullest who knew aught of her felt that if ever she awoke to any preference she would never stoop to mask it. She cared nothing for the opinion of any living being. She had no lover, only because she had no love.

Under her nonchalance and her occasional sentiments of sympathy with revolutionists, she was of an inexorably proud temperament; she would have liked to be an empress,—an empress such as was seen in earlier times, whose mere breath spoke the *fiat* of life and death. As it was, she could only vex the souls of men and kill orchids.

When she reached home, after driving until dusk, she passed through her boudoir to see if Paul had obeyed her. He had obeyed her implicitly: the windows were still wide open and the bitter biting air was streaming into the room, driving out before it all the heat from the calorifère; all the poor flowers were withered, as if a scorch from fire had passed over them, and the beautiful butterfly petals were mere shrivelled, shapeless leaves. It had been a pity, she thought, to have obeyed her so exactly; yet she knew very well that if he had not done so, Paul, despite his twenty-five years of service to the house of Napraxine, would have found himself outside her doors for evermore that night.

'Shut them now,' she said to him, as he waited for her commands, 'and take away all those baskets and bouquets.'

Paul knew her too well to dare to remark what he had thought all the afternoon, that it had been a sad waste of some fifty thousand francs' worth of blossoms. He closed the windows in silence. She passed on towards her dressing-chambers through the little library which divided the boudoir from them, the gayest and most coquettish of little libraries in appearance, with ivory bookcases ornamented by painted medallions of birds, a few white marble busts, and hangings of modern Gobelin tapestry; but a library by no means destitute of serious and philosophic works of some Latin authors, and of transactions of recent scientific research.

In the library, Paul, hesitating, ventured to approach her with a bouquet which was not harmed by the twilight frost.

'This was left a few moments ago,' he explained as he tendered it in some trepidation, uncertain whether he had done wrong to exclude it from the general massacre. She took it indifferently: it was very simple;—a bouquet of narcissus with a rim of white violets, nothing else. The name on the card with it was Othmar's. She smiled and took it with her into her dressing-room. It was the bunch of 'corn-cockles' for which she had wished.

'I did not do wrong,' thought Paul, with a sigh of relief. Then he smiled too as he recalled the winter in which the sender had been many times alone with his mistress in that little room where the orchids had now withered in their gilded baskets. 'It was he if it were ever anyone,' he thought; 'but I do not believe it has ever been anyone—yet.'

His knowledge of the world made him make the restriction, as he called one of his subordinates to sweep away all that rubbish, pointing to the poor murdered flowers, whose costly *corbeilles* would be one of his many perquisites.

She, meanwhile, was undressed, clothed in a loose gown of embroidered china silk, took a cup of tea, and slept peacefully in the perfumed warmth. She liked to come out of the frosty and foggy air, and lie still with the pleasant drowsiness caused by the contrast of the sharp evening wind and the atmosphere heated to 40° Réaumur. Physicians told her that so sudden a change was not wise or safe, but she laughed at them. 'What is pleasant is always wholesome,' she said, constructing new rules of hygiene, as she often did new rules of etiquette. She liked the warmth, the sense of repose, of languor, of voluptuousness, as a cat loves it, stretched on velvet, in still hot air. She slept now with perfect composure, dreamlessly, from the semi-stupor that driving against cold winds brings with it afterwards. Then, all at once, she dreamt of a lake half frozen, of dark tempestuous skies, of an open grave in the black water under the jagged drifting ice; and she awoke with a little unconscious cry to open her eyes on the mellow light, the satin hangings, the Saxe mirrors, the snowy bear-skins of her dressing-room, the little tray of silver and china, the bouquet of narcissus and violets near her.

'What a wretched dream! I, who never dream,' she said impatiently, as she stretched her limbs out on the white furs of her couch. Then she remembered Geraldine.

'Will he haunt me every time I go to sleep?' she thought, with a little shiver. It seemed to her altogether unreasonable and undeserved. She had never told him to go on the Gulf of S. Lawrence in the dangerous season before the ice was solid.

In an hour's time she took the bouquet of narcissus in her hand, and descended to her drawing-rooms. She wore the pink pearls that night, the little crown holding up her hair, raised like that of the portraits of Madame Tallien: she never wore her hair twice together in the same fashion. 'If you always wear your hair the same way, you have no imagination, and you are always suspected of a peruke,' she was wont to say.

Platon Napraxine seeing his despised gift thus honoured, was almost contented. In the *régime* of starvation, on which he had been kept so long, the smallest crumbs of condescension were eagerly seized by him.

She herself was in a gentle and gracious mood; she was not quite so merciless in speech as usual, but she was quite as charming. The Duc d'Aumale sat on her right hand, the English Ambassador on her left. Her airy laughter rang ever and again like silver bells; and Napraxine, even in the midst of the surprised gratitude with which he saw his pink pearls honoured by being worn, thought with a sense of depression and wonder: 'If I were to die to-morrow, would she care a whit more than she cares now for Ralph?'

CHAPTER XXXIX.

The telegram had merely said that Geraldine had been killed on the ice in the Gulf of S. Lawrence. There had been no details; but later on all the world learned that death had come to him in the freshness of his manhood by one of those trite accidents so common in North American waters in the beginning of winter, when the ice is still loose and detached, and is borne to and fro by the sullen waves which seem unwilling to endure its chains. He had been standing on an ice floe, off the Prince Edward Island, with Canadian hunters, seeking seals, when that portion of it which sustained them had suddenly broken away before they were aware of their danger, and, drifting with frightful rapidity, had borne them out to sea at the close of the short, bitter winter's day. Many on the shore were witnesses of the certain death to which they were carried, but no help was possible before the darkness of night came down,—the night which froze all human life left without shelter in it.

Where the floe went none knew; when the dawn broke there was no trace of its passage to be made out amidst the many masses of ice rocking, meeting, parting, crashing one upon another as the frost strove to bind beneath its iron hold the free will and the wild anger of the sea. Whether those who had been upon it had been drowned, or frozen to death, or borne out to mid-Atlantic, none could know; but on the third day the body of Geraldine and of two of the Canadian fishermen had been washed ashore off the New Brunswick coast: his features had been recognised by his own crew, and the tidings of his cruel fate had been sent to his mother and his sisters. He had been the only son of a high and honourable House. There was the grief which sorrowed without hope in the old north country halls, where a widowed mother wept for him, and a loyal and loving tenantry followed his body to its grave by the fair Yore waters.

One Tuesday evening, some two weeks later, when Nadine Napraxine returned home from the opera to change her gown for a ball at Prince Orloff's, there lay on her dressing-room table, amongst others, a letter of which the superscription was very familiar to her, and which moved her with a certain sense which was as nearly fear as it was possible for her temperament to know.

She herself had written to Geraldine's people, but no one of them had answered her until now that Evelyn Brancepeth did so. She broke the envelope and read the letter, standing in the costume of Venetian red embroidered with silver flowers, in which, at the opera that night, she had held all the eyes of the house upon her as she sat, careless, indifferent, half hidden behind her great red fan, the diamond butterflies which served in the place of sleeves trembling upon her shoulders.

'I know very well,' wrote Lady Brancepeth, 'that before the world you are wholly blameless. I know that my unhappy brother had no right to consider himself preferred by you. I know, were I speaking with you now, you would say with your chilliest manner that you had never honoured him with any encouragement to folly. But you will pardon me if I say that you are more blamable to me than you would be if you had loved him. I am a plain, stupid, unromantic Englishwoman, but even I can see that love excuses its own excesses: *l'amour prime le droit*. I could pardon a great passion if it even committed a great crime. But you have no passion, you have even no sentiment. You are sometimes amused, and you are sometimes—much more often—bored; and there the scale of your emotions rounds itself and ends. There may be someone who can, or who will, extend for you that narrow circle, though I very greatly doubt it; but it was entirely certain that poor Ralph had never any chance or any power to do so. He adored you, quite stupidly and hopelessly, but he never even knew how to say so in such a manner as could have touched you. He was very English, very *terre à terre*, and if he had never seen you he would have led a happy life enough; a commonplace one, no doubt, but one useful in his generation, and content with those simple joys which to a *raffinée* like you seem so absurd and so dull. But he did meet you; and ever afterwards life meant nothing to him unless it meant your presence, and your will. You had admitted him into the honour of a certain intimacy, which, in his blundering English way, he fancied meant all kinds of eventualities that it did not mean. No doubt his delusion was of his own creating, and of course he ought to have been prepared for his dismissal when he had become troublesome or tedious; but he was so unwise that he put all his heart into that which he should have understood was a mere *jeu de salon*; and you did not condescend to give him any warning. Why should you? you will say. Why, indeed, since his fate was as entirely indifferent to you as the bouquets that crowd your antechambers in Carnaval. It would have been so very easy for you, when first my brother ventured to show you what he felt, to banish him for ever with a decisive word; he would have been man enough to understand and to accept it; but you did not take that trouble, and the love of you grew—not perhaps precisely upon hope—but at least upon the tacit permission to exist. I scarcely know why I write all this to you, for you will not read it; only I have been your friend, so far as you allow any woman to call herself so, and I feel that whenever we meet in the world you will expect me to be so still, and I cannot. I must ask you to let us be strangers. No doubt, actually, you are innocent of my brother's death, but indirectly—even in a manner directly—you were the cause of it. You made his country, his family, his home life, his duties of all kinds, become no more to him than if he had never known land or kindred. The pain with which you filled him made him wander in an aimless unrest from place to place in an alien world with which he had no sympathy, and made him only too willing to die, that he might so throw off the fever of your memory. My dear Nadine, you are a woman of perfect honour, of high repute, of sensitive and unbending pride, and on the ermine of your delicate dignity there is no stain as yet. But for me, there is blood upon your hand. I can never take it in my own again. Let us be strangers.'

The letter was signed, and nothing more was added to it.

Nadine Napraxine read the lines through, word by word, and when she had done so, folded it up and put it aside, without irritation, but not altogether without regret. The frank, sincere, and at times rough words of Geraldine's sister had been welcome to her by their contrast with the false sweetness of the world's phrases, and she knew that she would lose her friendship with reluctance, and miss her surly honesty, with its uncompromising truths. But the letter seemed to her exaggerated, not in the best taste, even if, under the circumstances which inspired it, natural enough. Geraldine had perished by such an accident as every year costs scores of fishers' lives whenever the ice floes meet and sever in the half-frozen seas of the north. Why would they see her hand in it so clearly?

'It is just as they always see the finger of God where a horse stumbles at a post and rails, or when a pointsman is sleepy and does not hang out the red light,' she said to herself, with some impatient contempt. 'I am sorry, quite sorry myself, that he is dead, but I certainly never told him to get upon a block of ice in midwinter on the St. Lawrence. And it was quite as much Platon's doing as mine that ever he took the habit of coming about our house at all. Besides, if he had not been very stupid, as even his sister says, he would have understood *à demi-mot*; there is nothing on earth so tiresome as people who want things explained.'

Still, there were passages in the letter which touched her conscience, and reached that truthfulness in self-judgment which easily awoke in her.

'I suppose I am unkind—sometimes,' she thought, with a certain contrition. 'When they irritate me I really do not care what becomes of them. As long as they know how to please me I am always amiable. It is not my fault that their knowledge comes to an end too soon. It is their own poverty of style, of thought, of invention. If I were writing a dictionary, and had to define Man, I should say he was a limited animal, exceedingly limited. There is infinitely more variety about dogs.'

The very recollection of the excessive monotony of the human species made her yawn. She wondered if that monotony were the fault of civilisation; probably not. In a savage state, no doubt, instincts had been all alike, just as manners were all alike now. People were all dull, and because she found them so they considered her heartless. Poor Geraldine had been dull; dull in comprehension, in intention, in discernment; and just because she had found him so his sister wrote to her as if she were a murderess.

'Poor woman!' she reflected. 'She is always so disposed to see everything so terribly *en noir*. That is so English, too. They always have the fog in their eyes. I am not in the least like Lady Macbeth. I neither murder men, nor have my sleep murdered by them. It is natural that she should feel keenly the loss of her only brother, but it is absurd that she should lay the blame upon my shoulders, when she knows that if he had not wished to shoot seals—which is a barbarous pastime—he would most probably be alive now. As if a man could be wasting with despair, and yet care about seals! To be sure, it is very English. If an Englishman be hopelessly in love with any one, he generally goes a long way off and tries to kill a tiger or a moose. I do not see the connection of ideas between the sigh of passion and the steel of a gun barrel, but there must be some link of affinity for them, because they all do it. I prefer men like Othmar, who kill other men.'

Although she was all alone as these thoughts drifted through her mind while the letter of Lady Brancepeth lay amongst the litter of notes, cards, and invitations on her table, a momentary warmth came on her face as the name of Othmar recurred to her, and a certain bitterness of contempt came into her recollection as she remembered his marriage. If he had had patience, if he only had had patience, perhaps—perhaps—perhaps——

She would not have gone away with him, because in her world they did not do those things, and she would have always been too keenly afraid of an after-time of regret and weariness, but she might have accepted the gift of his life, and given him something of her own.

In his haste and wrath he had set up a barrier between them, but how frail it was! Only the timid, wistful youth of a girl! The imperial scorn of the Cleopatras of the earth rose in her before her meek, childlike rival.

What a coward he had been to shelter himself behind the frail rampart of a young girl's affection; affection which he did not appreciate, did not reciprocate, did not value!

A woman with a tithe part of the discernment and the experience which she possessed could cast the horoscope of Yseulte without any recourse to the stars for knowledge of the future. All that fresh and tender love would count for nothing, would avail nothing, would awaken no response. She would bear his children, and live in his houses, and be the object of all his careful outward observance, and that would be all. He would grow unspeakably weary of seeing her, of hearing her, of remembering her tie to him, and he would conceal his weariness ill or well, and be every day more and more galled by the necessity for concealment.

When Nadine Napraxine, after the ball, went to her own rooms that night, she had herself undressed by her women and wrapped in a loose bed-room gown, made of her favourite white satin, and lined with eider-down. She dismissed her women, and lay before the warmth of her dressing-room fire in that dreamy state between waking and sleeping which is the very perfection of repose. The softly-lighted chambers opened one out of another in a vista of rich subdued colour, ending in the bath room, where a lamp hung above a beautiful reproduction of the Venus of Naples. The rooms were so many temples to her own perfections, she was the Grace, the Muse, and the Venus herself of this perfect sanctuary, which no footfall of man had ever dared invade. As she reclined before the fire that night and glanced through her half-closed lids down the succession of chambers, which in the clear but delicate light had the glow of jewels, she thought how dull and empty they would have seemed to most women of her years without a lover's step coming silently and swiftly through the fragrant silence.

'Decidedly,' she mused, 'the *voix de la nature* says nothing at all to me. Is it because I have no heart, as they say? I do not think the heart has much to do with that kind of thing. I suppose I am cold, as they all cry out against me. Of all of them, there is no one I should care to see coming through those shadows; he would disturb me. The passions are coarse things. It is disgusting that there should not be two ways of love, one for Dona Sol and one for Manon Lescaut—for one's self and one's maid. But there are not. *On se rend, ou on ne se rend pas*; but when the submission is made Nature makes no difference between Cleopatra and a camp-follower.'

She sighed a little, inconsistently. She disdained alike the solicitations of the senses and the pleasures of the affections, and yet she was conscious of a certain coldness and emptiness in her life; she was not prepared to confess that what she needed was love, but a vague impression of solitude came upon her. She remembered the lips of Othmar pressed upon her wrist, how they had burned, how they had trembled!

Was it possible that the keenest joys of life lay, after all, in those follies which her temperament and her philosophies had classed with contempt amongst the excesses of wantons and the exaggerations of poets?

The purest maiden in her cloister could not have been colder than was Nadine Napraxine; to her the indulgence of the senses only meant an intolerable humiliation, an ignominious outrage; maternity itself had only been to her a long and hated and revolting burden, a sign of unendurable degradation, which offended all her pride and all her delicacy. The satyr had always seemed to her a much juster emblem of such instincts than any winged amorino.

'D'un être inconnu le contact passager'

could not rouse any desire or any sentiment in her.

And yet there were occasionally moments, fleeting ones it is true, when in the sublimated egoism of her indolent, ironical, artificial life, she had a vague impression of some possible passion which yet might arouse her to acknowledge its force; a tempestuous fancy swept over her, as a storm-wind may sweep over a parterre of tulips and azaleas, for stronger emotions, hotter enmities, dearer attachments, keener strife, than those which the polished inanities of her own sphere could yield to her. The emotion lasted with her very little time, but whilst it was there the eyes of Othmar always looked in memory into hers.

She who at will forgot everything had never forgotten the sound of his voice as he had pleaded with her. It had ever since haunted her with a vague imperfect sense of something missed, something lost, something in her own life incomplete and unattainable. She had not a doubt but that in time they would have wearied each other—fatigue was the inevitable shadow of all love—yet she had a pathetic regretfulness as for life incomplete, undeveloped, unshared, whenever she remembered that hers and his might have been passed together.

It had been only a sentiment; it never had risen to the form of desire, or ached with the pain of passion; but it had been a sentiment, vague, almost poetic; a wild flower of feeling which seemed of strange growth in the hot-house culture of her intelligence, and the rarified chill air of her many philosophies.

She had sometimes said to herself, 'I could have loved him.' In self-communion the conditional mood is never parted by more than a hair's breadth from the present. There were moments in the ironical, indolent, artificial life which usurped her time and thoughts in which she almost regretted that decision which had banished Othmar from her side and given him to another. The regret was as nearly a movement of the heart as she was capable of; but it was much besides that; it was the inquisitiveness of a *désœuvrée* incredulous that life could hold any great emotions for her; it was the impulse of a contemptuous courage to break through social laws which it despised; it was the desire of a woman lonely amidst her triumphs to find that key to the enjoyment of existence which, in some way or another, had slipped through her hands, and had never been discovered in its hiding-place.

'If I had been quite sure that he would have contented me!' she thought more than once.

If she had been quite sure, she would have surrendered everything, paused at nothing; it was neither daring nor generosity which were wanting in her; but she had not been sure, since she was never sure of herself!

CHAPTER XL.

A fortnight afterwards, the Prince and Princess Napraxine issued cards for a dinner, to meet the Emperor of all the Russias. The invitation came to the Hôtel Othmar at noon, as Yseulte sat at breakfast; she coloured a little as she saw it, and passed it across the table to her husband with a dozen other invitations. He glanced at them, put them aside, and spoke of something else. She hesitated a few minutes, then said timidly:

'Am I to accept it?'

'Accept which of them?'

'The Princess Napraxine's.'

He looked up with some displeasure at her tone; he answered quickly:

'Assuredly. Why not? You cannot leave it open as you do for a ball or a reception.'

She did not venture to say why. She coloured more and more, and remained silent.

'You have no plea for refusing invitations since you are not ill and are seen everywhere,' he said coldly. 'Besides, I thought you were acquiring the tastes of the world.'

She did not speak. She could not say to him: 'I cannot bear to be the guest of Madame Napraxine, because they tell me you have loved her as you never have loved me.'

Othmar glanced at her, and imagined what was in her thoughts. 'Perhaps that meddlesome Melville has talked to her,' he thought, with the ready suspicion of a man of the world of an ecclesiastic. He said, a little impatiently:

'My dear child, do not conceive animosities against people, or you will spoil your own sweetness of temper and make yourself disliked by your own sex. And do not fret yourself with imaginary antagonisms, which are altogether unworthy of you. When we are living in the world, we must abide by its rules of courtesy. I am wholly at a loss to imagine why you should be unwilling to accept this invitation; but as you are seen everywhere in this your first Paris winter, you cannot without rudeness refuse it. This is the only good that I have ever seen come out of society, that it compels us to subordinate our own inclinations to certain definite laws of good breeding.

Pray do not grow fretful; it was your beautiful serenity that I first admired, and loved.'

He hesitated a moment before the last word.

'I will remember,' she said gently; but without much effort she would have burst into tears.

He saw the effort, and it irritated him. He knew that he ought to have said to her, 'Follow your inclination and refuse, if you like.' But her wish to refuse it had annoyed him, and hurried him into a command to accept it from which he could not recede. And the charm of Nadine Napraxine was upon him, and had broken down all his wiser resolutions.

He looked across the table at Yseulte. She was as fair as the dawn, certainly; but she had no power over him; she did not beguile his time, or stimulate his wit, or stir his intellect; she did not, even after twelve months of possession, move his senses. She was a lovely child, most obedient, tender, and spiritual; but—she was not the mistress of his thoughts. She never had been, she never would be so.

'How stupid men are!' thought Nadine Napraxine that night. 'She is worth very much more than I am; she is both handsome and lovely; she is as harmless and guileless as a dove, and she adores him, a great deal too much; yet, perhaps one ought to say therefore, he cares nothing on earth for her; he will love me as long as his life lasts; he would do so even if I had the tremendous penalty-weight, as the racing-men say, of being his wife. I really do not know why it is that the noblest sort of women do not excite love. I wonder why it is? I asked my father once; he said, "Because the devil dowers his own daughters." But that explains nothing; we all know there is no devil; there are women—and women. That is all.'

As those thoughts drifted dreamily through her mind she was conversing all the while about classic music with a potentate who was no mean dilettante in melody, and she was looking down her table at the young face of Yseulte with a vague sort of pity which she could scarcely have explained,—such pity as in the gladiatorial arena some trained and irresistible *retiarius* might have felt at seeing some fair brave youth enter with the shield that was to be so useless and the sword that was so soon to fail; a pity which might be quite sincere, though it might never go so far as mercy. The faint jealousy which she had felt when, walking amongst the moonlit fields of Zaraïzoff, she had thought of Amyôt, had faded altogether the moment that she had met Othmar again. She knew, as women always know such things, that her power over him was unaltered and unalterable by any will of his own.

'When I choose,' she thought, 'he will leave her and she will break her heart. She will know nothing about such reprisal as a Parisienne should take; she will never be a Parisienne; she will always be a patrician of the *vieille souche*, which is quite another thing; she will always be an innocent woman, with a soul like a lily. She is afraid of me, and she dislikes me; she tries to hide it all she can, but she does not know how. Platon admires her; that is what he ought to have married; I dare say she would never have found him ugly or clumsy; he would have been her husband—that would have been enough to make him sacred; there are women like that. She adores Othmar, but she knows nothing about him; he is a little like Hamlet, and she is as much puzzled as Ophelia. Of course she would have worshipped any man who had prevented her being buried in a convent; she is as full of life as a lime-tree in flower. She is longing to look at me always, but she does not dare. She is quite beautiful, quite, but all that is no use to her. He knows it, but he does not care for it. He will keep her in his house and have children by her, but he will care no more for her than for Mercié's Andromache, that stands in his vestibule. Whether you are Venus or a Hottentot matters so little if a man do not love you; if you do not know how to make him love you. They always say a modest woman never does know how; but I do not think I am especially immodest, yet I know——'

The disjointed thoughts drifted through her mind without interfering with the current of her conversation. Metaphysicians may dispute the existence of two simultaneous trains of thought, but women know their possibility.

Her enigmatical victorious smile came on her lips as that consciousness soothed and stimulated her.

She had too much honour to make any deliberate project to seduce him from his allegiance. Her coquetries might be less merciful than many more guilty, but they had never ceased to be innocent in the world's conception of the term. The coldness with which Othmar had reproached her was still one of the most definite of her qualities. It was the amulet of her magic, the secret of her power. She was as yet a perfectly passionless woman, and as such ruled the passions of men.

'So, Othmar, like every one else, you find that marriage leads to the world, not to the hidden doves' nest of the poets?' said Nadine Napraxine after dinner, when her rooms had filled an hour before midnight, and her imperial guest had gone and left her free.

'I am afraid it is impossible to avoid following the mould of the society we live in,' replied Othmar. 'The hope of being original is one of the many illusions which we leave behind us with time.'

'I confess that I am a little disappointed in you,' she continued, with the smile of malice which he knew so well. 'I should have thought you would have had courage to live your own life, to avoid beaten paths, and to keep your lovely arum lily from the Breton woods out of our forcing-house. Allow me to say it in all simplicity and sincerity, she is most lovely. All Paris envies you.'

Othmar's face flushed as he bowed in acknowledgment. He did not reply. Though the habits of the world had taught him many such lessons, he found it hard to appear unmoved beside the woman he loved, and discuss with her that other whom he had wedded. She understood quite well the unwillingness and the embarrassment which he felt, and they made her but the more tenacious in pursuit of the subject she had selected.

'Heavens!' she thought, 'what children of Nature men always remain! They are unmanned if they meet a woman who recalls a love scene ten years old, whilst a woman would not move an eyelash if she encountered a score of lovers she had forsaken—no!—not if she had hired bravoes to kill them, and they knew it!'

Aloud she said, in her sweetest voice: 'I remember you were always so haunted with ideals. You must certainly have realised the most spiritual and the purest of them now. When I heard people say that you were going to shut yourself up in your country house in the Orléannais, it seemed to me perfectly natural, perfectly fitting; you never cared for society. Why should you contaminate your young wife with it? I thought you were going to show us that an idyllic life was still possible. We are all sad sceptics, but we should have believed *you*. Why did you lose so good an opportunity? To live in Paris, to receive and be received; any one can do that; *toute la gomme* does it; Amyôt ought to have given you something better.'

'To live in the country needs a clear conscience,' replied Othmar impatiently, not very well knowing what he said.

'I hope you have murdered nobody,' said his tormentor. 'Really, without compliment, I should have thought you were one of the few men who could have lived in the country without ennui. You love books, you like your own company, and you are not enamoured of that of others. Besides, it is really a pity to bring that young angel,—that clear-eyed saint,—into our feverish world. She will only lose that lovely complexion, and perhaps her health as well, learn a great deal of folly, and feel thirty years old before she is twenty. Why do you do it? It is heartless of you. Amyôt is her world.'

He did not attempt to reply.

She had spoken with sincerity, though her motive in speaking was not so sincere as her sentiment. Nadine Napraxine, who herself often regretted the premature womanhood which the manner of her childhood had brought so early to her, who often sighed restlessly, if disdainfully, for that innocence of mind, that freshness of heart which she had never enjoyed—the blue cornflower of Louise of Prussia, the green fields of Eugénie de Guerin,—felt at that moment the impulse of compassion which she expressed. It seemed to her, momentarily at least, cruel to have brought any creature so youthful and so easily contented by simple things, as Yseulte was, into the furnace of the world, where all simple tastes and fancies perish like a handful of meadow daisies cast into a brazier.

'And to have brought her near *me!*' she thought, with the singular union of disdain and of compassion with which she had looked for the first time at the face of the child in the salons of Millo. Whilst he remained silent she looked at him a little curiously, a little contemptuously; with no pity whatever for him.

'One day, when I was ten years old, I was in my father's study,' she continued with apparent irrelevance. 'I was very tiresome; he was dictating to three secretaries alternately, and I tormented him with questions. He was so good to me that he could never bear to turn me out; but he threw me an illustrated copy of "Gil Blas." I became as quiet as a mouse. I was entranced, delighted; I never spoke for two hours—but I do not know that I was the better for it afterwards. "Gil Blas" is not amongst the moral tales of children. I suppose he did not think of that; he only wanted to get rid of me.'

Othmar coloured with anger and self-consciousness. He knew very well that she meant to imply that he sent his wife into the world as Count Platoff had given his daughter 'Gil Blas.' Conscience would not allow him a disclaimer, even if a sense of ridicule in her reminiscences, apparently so ill-timed, had permitted him to make one.

'I do not know that I was any the better,' continued Nadine Napraxine in the same even, dreamy tones. 'But I do not know that I was any the worse. Everything depends on temperament. Oh yes, much more than on circumstance, let them say what they will. Temperament is like climate, a thing unalterable. All the forces of men will not make the Nile desert cold, or the Baltic shores tropical. It is so delightful to think that something escapes the carpentering of man! Do you know, when an earthquake asserts itself or a mountain kills people, I can never help saying to myself with pleasure—"Ah-ha! there is *something* left, then, that they cannot explain away, or regulate, or measure with their pocket-rule, and what a comfort that is!"'

She laughed a little, leaning back in her chair, slowly moving a fan which Watteau had painted for Larghillière.

'Madame Napraxine,' answered Othmar bitterly, 'has always occupied in life the position which Juvenal thought so enviable; she has always watched the tempest and the shipwreck from her own safe couch behind her casement.'

'Yes, I have,' she murmured, with a little sigh of self-satisfaction. 'It is so easy not to go out in bad weather.'

'May one not be overtaken by it?'

'Not if one have a good aneroid.'

'Let us leave metaphor,' she continued, after a pause; 'I know you believe in something like the Greek Erinnys; but you may believe me that there is nothing of the kind. We all make our own fates, or our temperaments make them for us. Destiny does not stalk about amongst us unseen, but irresistible, as I know you think it does. I believe there is nothing which befalls us, from a catarrh to a catastrophe, which, if we choose to be honest with ourselves, we may not trace to our own imprudence.'

'You cannot judge; you have never——'

'Never had a cold? Oh, indeed I have. If you were to listen to de Thiviers, I am a person on whom the most southerly wind should never be allowed to blow, for fear of its blowing through me and annihilating me; as for catastrophe——'

She paused a moment; across even her profound indifference there passed the memories of some dead men.

'Catastrophes,' added Othmar; 'catastrophes have not been lacking in the pageant of your life, madame; but I believe they have only been the shipwrecks seen through the windows of rose-glass.'

She was silent. Then she said slowly and in a low voice:

'You mistake if you think that I did not feel pain for the death of Seliedoff.'

Othmar bent his head. She saw that he did not believe her. The sense of being misjudged banished her momentarily chastened mood.

'But I was at the same time very much annoyed,' she continued. 'Tragedy always annoys me. It sets the asses of the world braying. No one ever pleases me by irrational or exaggerated actions. I am sorry, of course, but I cannot forgive the uproar which all conduct of—of that sort causes me. It always irritates me like the conflagration in the cantata of the 'Dernière Nuit de Sardanapale,' where the *grosse caisse* always roars and rolls so loud that all the music is lost, and one does not feel to care in the very least who may die or who may live.'

Then she rose and gave him a little smile.

'I assure you the *grosse caisse* is a mistake in a cantata!' she said as she passed him and left him, the subtle, voluptuous odour of the gardenias of her bouquet floating by him like the dewy odours of a midsummer eve.

He thought bitterly that he could comprehend how such a man as Joubert loved the scent of tube-roses till his death, because a woman once had taken a cluster of them from his hand twenty years before in a garden alley of the Tuileries.

It irritated him extremely that she should so exactly have suspected and penetrated the motive which had led him to desire that the life of the world should distract and occupy the young companion of his life. It was a motive of which he was acutely ashamed, which he could not endure to confess to himself, much less could bear to feel was subject to the observation of her unsparing raillery. Of all wounds which she could have reopened, none would have ached more keenly in him than his humiliating sense of how she, at the least, must know that the young girl who bore his name had no place in his heart; that she, at the least, must remember, as he remembered, those interviews with her at La Jacquemerille which had been so closely followed by his marriage. He might deceive all the world into the belief that he loved his wife—he could not so deceive her. His veins thrilled, his blood burned, as he recalled those two days in which his passion had been spoken to her in words whose utterance he himself could never forget. What had they sounded to her ear? Only, no doubt, like the *grosse caisse* which, symbolising death, agony, destruction, woe untellable, yet only seemed to her grotesquely forcible, jarring unpleasantly on the harmonious serenity of the symphony!

He forced himself not to follow her with his eyes as she moved away with that exquisite harmony of step and carriage which were due to the perfect proportions of her form, and he turned and sought out Yseulte herself.

She was in the music-room, listening absently to an andante of Beethoven's, surrounded by a little court of men no longer young, who cared nothing for Beethoven, but much for her youth and her unconscious charm of manner.

'Are you willing to come away?' he murmured to her when the andante was ended.

She rose with eagerness; to be in the Hôtel Napraxine was oppressive and painful to her.

He took her away unobserved, and drove homeward beside her in silence. He looked at her profile, fair and clear against the light thrown from without on the glass of the carriage window, and at the whiteness of her slender throat, with its collar of pearls, and hated himself because he could only think, with a shudder, 'All my life must I sit beside her, a living lie to her!'

'Yseulte,' he murmured suddenly; then paused: he felt a momentary impulse to tell her the truth, to say to her, 'I do not love you—God forgive me!—I love another woman; help me, my dear, and pity me; do not reproach me; I will do the best that I can by your life; love me always yourself if you can; I need it sorely. We may never be happy; but at least there will be no falsehood or secrecy between us. That will be much.'

The impulse was momentarily strong upon him; he took her hand in his and said once more with hesitation: 'Yseulte——'

Then he paused; long habit of reserve, a sensitive fear of wounding and of being wounded, the tenderness of pity for a blameless creature who adored him and who, if he spoke his thoughts aloud, would never lie in peace upon his heart again, all checked the words which had risen to his lips.

He sighed, kissed her hand, and murmured some vague caressing phrase. The moment passed; the impulse of confidence and candour lost strength and courage. 'It would be cruel,' he thought. 'Since I have made my burden, let me at least have courage to bear it alone.'

It seemed to him unmanly and ungenerous to lay any share or shadow of it on this young life, which owed all its peace and light to ignorance of the truth. She was deluded, but she was happy: he let her be. He shrank from arousing her; he shrank from hurting her; she was like a child, doomed to starve on her awaking, but whilst she slept, dreaming, with a smile, that she was fed by bread from heaven.

CHAPTER XLI.

The Paris season seemed to all her world to have gained new brilliancy with the advent of the Princess Napraxine. The opening of that most desired and exclusive of all houses was an event of supreme import in the hierarchy of society, and she herself had returned from her self-inflicted exile in the North more disposed than usual for its frivolities and graces, more willing than usual to deign to see and be seen, more general in her courtesies, more amiable and benignant in her condescensions. When she chose, she could fascinate women scarcely less completely than she did men, and she did so choose this year of her reappearance from Russia. She was less capricious, less inexorably exclusive, less merciless in her ironies; those who knew her nature best concluded that something had pleased her; no one knew what. She, who had no secrets from herself as sillier people have, confessed frankly to herself that what pleased her was what her fine penetration had discovered at a glance, the first moment that she had entered the Hôtel d'Othmar.

'All the virtues are there, no doubt,' she had said to herself, 'and all the qualities and all the charms, but Love—où va-t-il se nicher?'

Love, she saw, was absent.

She had a curious sentiment towards the young mistress of that gorgeous house. She admired her; she thought her type pure and lofty, her manners most high bred, if a little too constrained, her face lovely; she had a sort of pitying regard for her; the glance of the girl's eyes moved her to compassion as those of an antelope will do the hunter, who nevertheless plunges his knife into its velvet throat; but she was not more dissuaded by her pity than the hunter is by his to desist from her intentions.

The waning of the slight affection which he had ever been able to give his young wife, the growing constraint of her manner to him and before him, the visible chillness which had fallen on their life together since that December night when she herself had arrived in Paris were all plain enough to her unerring perceptions, however slight might be the outward signs of that separation which was only not estrangement, because on the one side there was a devotion so timid, grateful, and constant that it could not be estranged.

Her world observed that she treated Yseulte with much more kindliness than it was common with her to show to women so young. Whenever she spoke of her, or to her, she always used some phrase which was gracious or flattering, with that most subtle and delicate flattery of which she had the secret as well as she had those of the most cruel ironies and insinuations; the extreme charm of her flatteries, as the intense sting of her cruelties, always lay in the fact that they contained a visible truth; they were not the mere offspring of invention.

Yseulte did not show to equal advantage when she received them; she was always embarrassed, even almost rude, so far as rudeness was possible to one nurtured in all the grand traditions of French patrician courtesy. In her own heart the child suffered excruciating mortification whenever the one woman whom she knew her husband had loved—did love—met her with sweet and praiseful words. She had all the exaggerated honesty of exceeding youth; she could not believe that sincerity permitted the sincere to smile on what they hated, and almost—almost—she hated this exquisite woman who was so gracious to her. It became an absolute dread upon her lest she should meet the one person who had this power to make her feel insignificant, ignorant, and awkward: a power never expressed, never even hinted at, yet lying beneath all those pretty phrases which the Princess Napraxine addressed to her or spoke before her. Her own innocent pleasure in these new pleasures of the world was marred by the constant apprehension of meeting her one enemy, who did not even give her the frank offence of an enemy, but always approached her with the smiling grace of a friendship the insincerity of which her own sincere instincts detected. The routine of their world brought them in almost perpetual contact, and Yseulte felt her presence before she saw her, and was conscious of a nervousness which she could not conquer, though she strove to conceal it. There was no one to whom she dared to speak of what she felt, and she was indeed ashamed of it. Youth dies a hundred deaths in silence in these unavowed antagonisms and apprehensions. If she had ventured to confess what she felt to Othmar, she would have ceased to be haunted by these vague terrors; but there was a look in his face whenever the name of Nadine Napraxine was spoken before him, which told her she herself must never speak it in blame or in fear. A chill and desolate consciousness had by degrees stolen upon her that they were right who said her husband loved this other woman as he never had and never would love herself. She said nothing to anyone, not even in the confessional; but a coldness like frost seemed to have come over her glad, warm, and grateful life just opened like the primroses in spring.

The day after he had left that simple bouquet of narcissus and white violets, Othmar had called at the Hôtel Napraxine. It was not her day, but she was at home and received him; it was the twilight hour so favourable to dreams, to confidence, to familiarity; when he had left the house he was conscious that he had done an unwise thing, perhaps even an unmanly thing; but he had been for the moment almost happy, which he had not been for a year.

They had not been even alone; but the sound of her voice, the languid glance of her eyes in the dim half-light, the music of her slight, low laugh, had all thrilled his veins with a thousand memories of passion and of hope; he had said to himself, 'I will never go back,' but he had gone back, and he knew that life would only count to him in future by the moments when he should return. In the evening which followed on his visit he was, quite unwittingly, colder and more preoccupied than Yseulte had ever seen him; he was even for once almost irritable. She looked at him wistfully. Friederich Othmar, who was present there, thought to himself in futile fury: 'That sorceress has bewitched him once more. In another twelvemonths' time, if he be not her accepted lover he will have shot himself. This poor fair child would cut her heart out of her breast to serve him; but she will grow less and less to him, less and less, every day. It is no fault of hers. He never cared for her, and she has no philtre of which she can make him drink. Innocent women do not brew them. Poor sweet fools! They can only pray!'

The old man had never cared for these women before; but now he did care. His heart which had been so cold all his life melted towards Yseulte.

Why could not Othmar be content with his *coin du feu?* When the Baron came into her apartment and saw the tall figure of the girl, with her fair head carried with a little droop like a flower's after rain, he was every day more and more angry to find her husband so seldom there. Yseulte seemed to him to have in herself all those beauties and qualities which should be sweetest in the eyes of a man. But she was left alone, very constantly alone.

To one who had loved her she would have been full of interest, of surprises for the imagination, and of nascent character for influence to work upon; but to Othmar she was only a child, tame, quiet, without power to arrest or to excite him.

In the presence of Nadine Napraxine every fibre of his being was thrilled and awake, every nerve of his mind and body was alternately soothed and strung; her discursive and ironical intelligence seemed to light up the universe of thought, and every syllable she spoke, every slight gesture, smile, and suggestive glance, were fuller of meaning and more appealing at once to the intellect and the senses than hours of effort and provocation from other women. When he passed from her presence into that of Yseulte it was as though he passed from the marvellous intricacies of the passion music of *Tristan und Isolde* to the simple peace and prayer of a Gregorian chaunt sung by a child chorister. The latter was not without beauty of its own; beauty harmless and holy; but which had no power to move him.

Little by little his caresses grew fewer, his attentions grew rarer to his wife; he was always full of courteous observance and unremitting kindness to her as before; but the times were rare in which he sought her alone—the evenings few in which he entered her apartments.

His whole remembrance, desires, and adoration were with Nadine Napraxine. He imagined that he entirely concealed his weakness from the world and from Yseulte; but as the weeks passed on and the opportunities of society brought him continually into the presence of the one woman whom he loved, the magical influence of her dominion began completely to absorb and to subdue him afresh. He still abstained from any intimacy at her house; he still most rarely visited her or directly sought her, but all the indirect occasions to be in her presence which the routine of their world afforded he accepted and looked forward to with an eagerness which he imagined was wholly unsuspected by others. When she was entertained at his own hotel he was studiously distant in his courtesies, and though he did not betray it, he was embarrassed by the honest and cordial regard which her husband showed to him.

Friederich Othmar would very much have liked to speak his mind on the subject to his nephew, but he felt that he had no possible pretext to do so, for Othmar was perfect in his manner to his young wife and constant in his kindness and solicitude for her. The elder man felt that he could not with decency split straws about imaginary wrongs when he himself had been always so incredulous of the sorrows of the affections. So long as Othmar refused her nothing, inflicted no slight on her publicly, and never said a syllable to her that was unkind or uncourteous, it was impossible for anyone to call him to account for mere fanciful offences which, however real might be the suffering they caused, had no substantial ground or root.

'He would laugh at me,' thought the Baron, and the whole philosophy of his life made any possible ridicule on grounds of sentiment intolerable to him even in idea. He was, moreover, conscious that Othmar would do more than laugh, and united to his impatience of his nephew's errors and caprices was a reverence for him as the chief of the House, which was still stronger than any other feeling. So might a loyal prince of blood royal see in his nephew a man most blameable, full of faults and of inconsistency, yet see in him also his sovereign, whose very errors or failures he was bound, for sake of their common race and of his sworn supremacy, to defend.

'Othmar can do no wrong in your sight,' said Nadine Napraxine once, with the smile that the Baron hated.

'Nor could the Roi Soleil in the sight of his family,' he responded, with a tone that was the reverse of amiable, 'yet there were lovely ladies on the terraces of Marley and Versailles who must have tried their patience and their faith sometimes.'

'Can faith and patience be said to exist unless they are tried?' said his tormentor. 'And I should think that the Treaty of Utrecht tried both much more than his preferences, which could not matter in the very least to them.'

Friederich Othmar was silent, twisting his white moustaches irritably. He would have liked to say many things to her, but he dared not; he did not know enough; and Othmar, implacably incensed, would have quarrelled with him then and for ever had he ventured to interfere.

He who had intelligence enough to appreciate the spirituality and unworldliness of Yseulte's nature, who had been first touched by her unlikeness to all the young girls of his world, by her serious and elevated character and her simple unostentatious piety, felt a sting of shame at his own motives when he realised how much he sought to make her like all other women, how much he trusted to frivolous temptations to console and to absorb her.

'In doubt do nothing,' he knew well was one of the golden legends of the world's wisdom. If she had sought advice or sympathy, her doubts and her fears might have been soothed in a measure. Her confessors would have given her the same counsel as that worldliest of men, Friederich Othmar. They would have entreated her not to fret her life out over mere sorrows of the emotions and the imagination; they would have hinted that she was exceptionally happy if she had no more to bear than an inconstancy of the mind and of the fancy; they would have bade her trust to her youth, to her own strength of affection, and to her place in his house and in his life, to give her ultimate supremacy in the thoughts and the heart of her husband. But even in the sanctity of the confessional she chose rather to commit the sin, for sin it was in her sight, of hiding all her inmost feelings and keeping silence on all her most rebellious impulses rather than speak of Othmar with any words which might imply suspicion, blame, or reproach to him. Her convent life had given her such little knowledge of human nature, her sensitive reserve of character left her so entirely without counsellors or friends, that she was altogether alone in the bewilderment of this world which had at first seemed to her at once a pageant and a paradise, but which, now that her soul was haunted by one poignant dread, only appeared to her filled with cruel problems, incomprehensible temptations, strange confusions and humiliating motives. To her, only one friend was possible, her husband; to him alone would her timidity and her honour have permitted her to confide all her pathetic fears, all her innocent secrets; but Othmar never sought her confidence. Treating her with the gentleness of a man to a child, with the respect of a gentleman for what he wholly reverences, and is always willing to protect and please, he yet remained as distant from her in true confidence and sympathy as any stranger ushered into her drawing-rooms, whose face she had never seen before.

Naturally unselfish, Othmar had yet unconsciously dropped into the habit of one intense selfishness; he wrapped himself in his own thoughts as in a domino, and drew each day more and more closely about him that reserve which spared him all the trouble of reply, all the ennui of interrogation. The continual demands which his great position in the world made upon his time gave him continued excuse for being alike occupied and absorbed. Often the whole day passed without her receiving more from him than a few brief gentle phrases of greeting or adieu.

But he had provided her with every possible means of enjoyment and of self-indulgence, and it did not occur to him that amidst all her luxury the heart of the child remained empty and hungered.

'He treats her as he would treat a mistress to whom he had grown utterly indifferent,' thought Melville, often observing him with anger. 'He surrounds her with every conceivable kind of luxury and distraction, and he leaves her alone amidst it. Does he think that a girl of her years wants nothing more than toilettes, horses, jewels, and *bibelots*? Does he suppose that at seventeen the heart is dead, and that the sentiments and the desires have said their last word? Does he believe that she will want nothing more of love than a chill embrace now and then, *pro formâ*? He leaves her at once so free and so starved, that were she any other woman in the world she would use her liberty in such wise that he would live to bitterly repent his neglect. But she is of the old time, the old school; she will keep silent and faithful; she will bear his children with the meekness and the resignation of the lambing sheep in spring-time; and she will rear them with courage, wisdom, and devotion. But she will not be happy, though probably the world will always envy her; and she will be less to him—less, less, less,— with every year which passes. In the end they will be total strangers, and she will accept that strange sort of widowhood—the saddest of all—as patiently as she accepted maternity and its pains. The cloister is out of date, perhaps, as they say, but the fact remains that there are natures for which, whether in or out of the cloister, life means crucifixion.'

Melville strove to do what he could to restore peace to her; but it is difficult to administer any efficacious medicine when no disease is admitted by the sufferer to exist. The extreme sensitiveness and the power of silent suffering in Yseulte baffled her well wishers, whilst it assisted those who did not wish her so well. When he, with his tact at suggestion, contrived to give her some hint that human love must always be accepted as a thing imperfect, that in every human life there must come disillusions, trials, and regrets, and that none of these need bring wretchedness with them if they be met with faith and patience, Yseulte listened to him with her usual courteous reverence, but felt bitterly that beneath his carefully chosen words, which were dropped with such elaborate assumption of hazard, as upon some general and impersonal subject, there were hidden both counsel to her and apprehension for her. She resented both with that hauteur which the blood of the de Valogne had given her; and he desisted from his efforts, afraid to do hurt where he washed to do good.

'After all,' he thought, 'one's fears for her may be wholly chimerical. Othmar is a man of honour, and Madame Napraxine is as chaste as snow,—according to report. It is true, her chastity has been as perilous and as cruel as the immoralities of others. But I think, even if to Othmar she should be not so cold, and be even more fatal than usual, his young wife may have charm enough to keep him faithful, or at least to win him back to fidelity.'

But though he tried thus to reassure himself, he did not succeed. He had learned much of the wisdom of society in his forty years of priesthood; he had been the favourite ecclesiastic of the great world, and he had seen much of its delicate and capricious women, of its unstable and unhealthy passions, of its irksome and disregarded ties; and he saw in the position of Yseulte many possibilities of error and unhappiness, little likelihood of a future of peace. Never within his memory, with its innumerable records of human destinies, had he ever seen simplicity, innocence, and devotion victorious over finesse, experience, and egotism; never within his memory had either the confessional or the drawing-rooms afforded him any precedent by which he could hope that the love which gave its all unreservedly and adoringly with both hands, would ever be conqueror over the seduction which provoked every desire and granted none, sacrificed nothing and expected all. Melville had always seen the egoist supreme in the conflict of life; his knowledge did not disturb his faith, it only made him the more convinced that there must be some future world in which all these wrongs would be set right; but it saddened him despite himself, and, despite his hope of ultimate compensation, he could not help whenever he could aiding the weak against the strong.

'If everything is done by the will of God, why do you try and alter it?' said Friederich Othmar to him once, with just sarcasm.

Melville was conscious that he was illogical, but he could not resist his own English love of fair play; it did not seem to him that as the world was made innocence and unselfishness ever obtained any chance of justice.

'It must be granted,' he thought mournfully once, also unable to resist his own clear-sightedness and its conclusions, 'it must be granted that both innocence and unselfishness are too often inconceivably, irremediably, stupid, and throw their best cards on the table and follow will-o'-the-wisps, and break their limbs over every obstacle which a little skill and coolness would enable them to negotiate.'

The keen eyes of Aurore de Vannes saw what Othmar did not see; that since the arrival of the Princess Napraxine her young cousin had no longer the single-hearted and buoyant happiness of the early months of her marriage, that her face was often melancholy, her gaze wistful, her manner constrained.

But her reflections were precisely contrary to those of Melville.

'She is fortunate beyond everything,' said the Duchesse to her intimate friends. 'He gives her all she can wish for, as if he were Haroun Alraschid, and he leaves her entirely to herself, because he is not in the least in love with her. Can anyone imagine a more enviable position?—to be seventeen years old and have all the Othmar millions at your back, and to enjoy such an absolute liberty that your husband never asks you even where you spend your days? Only she is such a baby still, so very full of all her convent fancies, so scrupulous, and proud, and old-fashioned, that I suppose she will never enjoy herself as she might do. She was ruined by those women at Faïel, and by the austerities and prejudices of the old Marquise. If she only knew it, her position might be the happiest in the world.'

'Will it not be as I said?' asked the Duc, her husband, triumphantly many a time. She always answered him irritably:

'If a woman prefer to be miserable she always can be; men will always furnish her with the materials. But in this case you may be quite sure it is merely a girl's romance and disappointment with marriage, which she expected, as they all do, to be a primrose path whilst it is only a common highway.'

'The highway can be varied by *étapes*,' murmured the Duc de Vannes.

He himself watched with unkind satisfaction the little cloud which had come in the serene heaven of Yseulte's fate. It might betoken but an April shower, or it might bring in its wake a tempest. When he had seen Nadine Napraxine arrive in Paris he had said to himself, 'Adieu les marguerites!' The daisies were simple treasures of the spring; they would have no charm beside the hothouse flower. As his little daughter had said, he had bet heavily on the chances of Yseulte's marriage, and he watched the unfolding of the leaves of fate with the impatience of the gambler added to the unacknowledged malice of a personal pique. In the frequent opportunities which both society and relationship afforded him he dropped the gall of many a vague insinuation, worded with tact and finesse, into the troubled peace of her thoughts. He had too much skill and too much good taste to permit himself to speak either Othmar's or Nadine Napraxine's name directly, but he had not been so long schooled in the cruelties of the world without having learned the art of suggestion in its most merciless and its most subtle shapes. He never said so in any clear form of words, yet he contrived to convey to her his own conviction and the conviction of society that she counted for nothing in her husband's existence. All his delicately-hinted compassion, all his vaguely-worded indignation, the mere light jests with which he strove to amuse her, all contained that drop of acid which burned its way into the pure gold of her affections, and remained with her long after he had left her presence.

She always summoned fortitude enough to repress any sign of the harm he did to her; but the effect of it was for that reason the more baneful. Sorrows and doubts, which pass away when a woman can weep for them at her mother's knees, or in her sister's arms, grow strong and cruel in solitary meditation and the nurture of thoughts unconfessed.

One night at a great fête the Duc de Vannes approached her and said to her with a smile:

'How preoccupied you are, my cousin! I never should have thought that anyone so young would look so grave at a ball. Really, you make one fear that after all you were wrongly turned from your vocation, and would have been happiest in the cloister, much as the world would have lost.'

'The world would have lost nothing,' answered the girl, a little bitterly. 'The world and I have no affinity.'

'That is only an idea. In a few years you will habituate yourself to——' he paused and added with meaning, 'to many things which seem to you harsh and cold. Penelope nowadays, if she spin at all to console herself for abandonment, only weaves the web of *flirtages*——'

Yseulte coloured at the insinuation contained in the phrase. Her heart was too full for her to trust herself to answer. Did all these people know, as she knew, that her husband had never loved her?

'You are *trop taillée à l'antique*,' said de Vannes with a little impertinence. 'Do you think you are ever thanked for all this exclusive devotion which does not permit you to smile at a ball? Do not be angered, Yseulte. I should be glad if I could persuade you that it would be much wiser to smile often—and smile on others. Men are ungrateful, my cousin. The spaniel love is not what moves them most.'

'I do not know why you should say this to me,' she murmured with embarrassment and offence. 'You presume too far on our relationship——'

'Pardon me!' said the Duc very humbly. 'My indignation is apt to outrun my prudence. I do not like to see—any one—passively accept neglect. Neglect should be avenged. It is the only way in which it can be transformed into allegiance.'

Yseulte made a courageous effort to conceal her knowledge of the drift of his words.

'I cannot tell what you allude to,' she said coldly. 'Nor do I see why you should feel any anger for which you are not asked.'

'In the last century,' continued de Vannes, as though he had not heard her, 'there was a woman called Lescombat; she was very beautiful and had many lovers; she incited them to many crimes. One of them, Mongeôt, was condemned to be broken on the wheel for one of these crimes. He could have cleared himself if he had revealed her name; but he never did. He died on the wheel silent. She went to the Place de Grêve and smiled to see his tortures. 'Il ne fallait pas moins que cela pour faire rougir Mongeôt!' she cried so loud that he could hear her: he had always been very fair and pale. But he died mute, nevertheless. It is women like the Lescombat, my cousin, who are loved like that. Pauline de Beaumont, the very flower and perfection of womanhood, was only allowed as a reward for her devotion to follow her lover at a distance like a dog and die in Rome. It is always so.'

A chill passed over the girl as he spoke. She said wearily:

'Madame de Beaumont was as nature and religion made her; she could not have rivalled your Lescombat if she had wished.'

Then she rose and went away from him.

When she returned home to her own rooms, where she was now too often left as solitary as though she had been in her nun's cell at Faïel, she fell upon her knees before her crucifix and sobbed bitterly: she had seen that night how wistfully, and with what unconsciously revealed longing and regret, the eyes of Othmar had followed every movement of her rival.

To her ignorance, Nadine Napraxine was a woman as cruel, as evil, as terrible as the murderess Lescombat of whom the Duc de Vannes had spoken. All the innumerable intricacies of line, and the delicate half-tints of which such a character as hers was composed, made a study far beyond the girl's power of analysis, even had any such power been left to her in the confusion and the fever of her thoughts. She only saw in her a sorceress, whose merciless will and irresistible seduction drew her husband from her as the Greek ships of old that passed to the world of the east were drawn out of their safe straight road by the loadstone rocks of the Gulf of Arabia. A sense of entire helplessness and of unending despair came upon her in those glad sunlit flower-filled Parisian days when all the pomp and pleasure which the great world could give were continually around her. If ever timidly and ashamed she ventured to reveal anything which she endured in the sanctity of the confessional, her confessor, an austere and fanatical recluse, always met her with the reply that, having turned as she had done from the paths of religion, she only met with her just retribution if the golden apples of terrestrial life, for which she had abandoned spiritual things, changed to ashes between her lips. She received no compassion from him and little consolation; she followed meekly the course of self-mortification he traced out for her; and, day by day, her cheek grew paler, her eye heavier, her step more slow and joyless.

She suffered as only a nature can suffer which is too sensitive to seek comfort in revealing itself, and too unused to the ways of the world to be able to find either distraction or compensation. No tortures would have wrung from her the confession of what she felt; she was ashamed of the passionate and piteous jealousy of which she was conscious; she thought it an offence against her husband and her God. But she could not resist its inroads into her peace; it grew and grew, and its insidious fires spread farther and farther in her simple soul, as a cancer spreads in healthy flesh.

She felt no sense of wrong; even in her own thoughts she uttered no reproach against him. In her own sight she was so utterly his debtor that she had no title to complain, even though he should wring her very heart with desertion. But a sickening despondency stole upon her little by little; each week brought with it some clearer sense of counting for nothing in his life, some sharper consciousness that she had no real place in his affections. Her perceptions, suddenly and cruelly aroused by the knowledge that he loved another woman than herself, became preternaturally keen in instinct and second-sight. She could tell in an instant, by the expression of his features, when he had seen her rival or when he had failed to meet her. Her mind, lately so ignorant of all the meanings of the world's babble, grew fatally alive to all its insinuations, its hints, its allusions, whenever these in aught concerned Nadine Napraxine. Her ear brought to her the faintest and most distant whispers in which the dreaded name was spoken. She became aware of the meaning of Othmar's glance, animated or absent, according as Nadine Napraxine was within his sight or not. She grew sensitive to all the different inflections of his voice, in which expectation, disappointment, pleasure, mortification, or impatience spoke. She was as susceptible to every change in him as the mercury to the frost and to the sun. Her whole existence was consumed in her study of him.

The self-restraint and the silence to which her early years had been trained, made her perfectly capable of repressing every outward sign of what she felt. Othmar saw no alteration in her; he saw that she went eagerly into the world, and imagined that she, like all women, had learned to enjoy its frivolities. She was always calm, docile, cheerful; she had at all times a graceful answer to those with whom she spoke, an admirable manner in whatever scene she was placed in. He never divined how, beneath the serious smile on her mouth which served to hide the aching, wistful doubts and fears of her still childlike heart, how, beneath the pretty stateliness and gravity which he had first admired at Millo, and which never altered in her, there throbbed the poignant pain of a timid and impassioned affection—wasted.

If he had loved her, he might have seen something of it, little as men are able at any time to read the soul of a woman; but he was only kind to her, gentle to her, faithful—as yet—to her. He never loved her, and so all that wistful, lonely suffering went on and grew greater and greater unguessed by him. When he sat by her side in the opera-house, all he saw was Nadine Napraxine on the opposite side of the theatre; when he entered a ball-room, or a music-room, or a drawing-room before a dinner, all he looked for were the dark, languid, luminous eyes of the woman he adored, and when he met their glance, and saw across a crowded salon the irony of her slight and subtle smile, he only lived for her.

CHAPTER XLII.

This duel, if duel it could be called, since all the science and almost all the advantages were on one side, passed constantly in the presence and beneath the eyes of Othmar. But he was blind to it with the shortsightedness of a man; he was, even, more than once irritated by what he thought was an excess of kindness, an unusual interest, shown by the woman whom he loved to his wife. He hated to see them near each other. He scarcely disguised his restlessness when he noted any approach to intimacy between them. The remembrance of those two mornings at La Jacquemerille were for ever with him. He could not pardon Nadine Napraxine that she appeared so entirely to ignore their memory. True, he thought bitterly, it was she who had betrayed him, and it is always the betrayed who remembers, the betrayer who forgets. Had he said so much to her she would have answered: 'My friend, I did not betray you; I only told you I would reflect. I did reflect; if the result of my reflections was adverse to you, it was your misfortune perhaps, but it was also your fault.'

Once or twice Melville endeavoured to induce Nadine Napraxine to speak of the young girl of whose destinies he considered her the arbitress, but he never succeeded.

'She is very beautiful;' she always answered with that talent in selecting what she could say truthfully, which was not the least of her wisdom. She added a few more words of eulogy, neither critical nor exaggerated; she did not permit him to have any glimpse of the consummate scorn joined to the sincere compassion with which she regarded the wife of Othmar, every one of whose emotions she read as though she read them in a book every time that the voice of Yseulte changed in greeting her or the girl's tell-tale colour rose, or faded, whenever she herself entered a room or looked at her across a theatre.

No one of all her lovers had ever been so completely mesmerised by her power as was this girl who held the name, the home, the honour of Othmar, whilst she herself held all his memory, all his desires, all his mind and heart and life.

It was the fascination of the ophidian for the dove. It gratified her sense of dominion, and aroused all her more cruel instincts. The reluctant fascination which she exercised over Yseulte; the visible effort with which the girl strove to escape from it and failed; the magnetism with which her gaze was riveted and her ear strained to follow every movement, to catch every utterance of her foe; that helplessness, that unwilling, yet powerless, subjugation, excited all which was coldest, most contemptuous, most inexorable, in the soul of the woman in whose veins ran the blood of the assassins of Paul. That clairvoyance which is the gift of all rare intelligences, made her as conscious of all the bewildered thoughts which thronged the mind of Yseulte as though she saw them in the magic crystal of a sorcerer. She knew how, when she looked at the girl carelessly, smilingly, over the feathers of her fan or the flowers of her bouquet, across the sea of light of the opera-house, the whole soul of her innocent rival shrank and trembled within her, even whilst the natural courage, and resolution, and pride, of the de Valogne blood forced her to endeavour to resist, and enabled her to succeed in concealing, the fear and trouble which she felt.

'She is brave,' said Nadine Napraxine to herself with respect; but all the scorn which was in her made her add, without pity, 'but what a child!— how foolish!—how transparent!'

In that continual flux and reflux of society which incessantly brings together those of the same world and allows them to see each other perpetually, even though they remain strangers, the occasions were frequent, almost daily, in which she could study this poor aching heart, which was laid as bare to her as though Yseulte had had a mirror in her breast, and, for no victory and no caprice of her life, had she ever been so interested *de se faire belle* as now, when she was conscious that her imperial charm, her nameless irresistible powers of seduction, had thrown their magic net over the life which had most cause of all on earth to fear her own.

If he had known that she had suffered thus, his compassion and his sense of honour would have been aroused and have taken alarm; but he was blind to it, as men dominated by an exclusive passion are blind to all outside it. His principles and his good taste would have made him his own most inexorable censor had he been in any act of his life faithless, in the gross meanings of the word, to the young life which he had united to his own. But he did not consider that a love which he pressed like a knife into the depths of his heart, and of which he believed he gave no outward sign whatever, did any wrong to Yseulte. She was still so young; she had all she desired; she would have children about her in other years; she was of that docile, feminine, unimpassioned nature which is easily content with the placid affections of the natural ties. He did not think that he betrayed her because, all unknown to her, he cherished in the depths of his own soul a bitter, cruel, hopeless, and yet most exquisite and most enduring passion. He had given her all which the world can give to any human creature; he did not realise that his lips were chill when he kissed her, his eyes indifferent when they glanced at her, his speech to her too often absent and conventional, his caresses too often forced, mechanical, and without any throb of warmth.

He knew well that if he were wise, even if he were faithful in intent to his wife, he would leave Paris whilst Nadine Napraxine was in it. His many possessions could have given him a hundred facile excuses for absence, and Yseulte would have gone willingly wherever he had chosen to take her. But he did not obey his conscience; he was swayed by his pride, which would not allow him to let the world say that he retreated before his sorceress, and he was held by that power which a great love exercises over the judgment and the volition. The mere glance of her eyes had fascination enough to destroy all his resolutions, and draw him into absolute oblivion of everything save herself. His passion for her was one of those which absence and denial intensify. He would make the arrangements of his whole day subordinate to one slight chance of meeting her for a moment in a crowd, of seeing her pass at a distance beneath the boughs of an avenue. He had received a mortal affront, a merciless insult, and yet he forgave them both; he was with her once more, he had no sense except of that one ecstasy. He was weak as a reed in her hands; he could have flung himself at her feet and kissed them. He knew that manliness, dignity, honour, duty, self-respect, all ought to have forbidden him to cross her threshold, but he was indifferent to them; they were mere names, without power, almost without meaning, for him. They had no more control over him than threads of silk upon the neck of a horse which has broken loose. She was before him, the one woman who was beautiful, beloved, and desired by him; and he realised that it had been of no use to try and cure a delirious fever with a simple draught of sweet herbs, as Melville had once said.

His own wife was nothing to him; the wife of Napraxine was all. He despised and hated himself for his inconstancy where his fealty bound him, for his fidelity where he had only received light mockery and cruel provocation. But he could not change his nature, and the education which life had given him had contained no lesson in the art of self-denial. The world had always been at his feet; his desires had always been gratified and his wishes forestalled; he had never been used to subjugate his own inclinations; and this, the first evil which had ever tempted him, began to assail him with increasing force with every day which brought him within sight of the one woman whom he adored. She knew his weakness as she knew that of every human being who ever approached her, and she had no compassion for it. A man who had done her the insult of presuming to seek elsewhere consolation for her own indifference, had no mercy from her in his failure; he had offended her in the only vulnerable portion of her character, her supreme love of exclusive dominion. She was not vain with any common vanity, but the instincts towards absolute mastery were strong in her; whoever thwarted those instincts, always repented his temerity in dust and ashes. Each step which Othmar made towards resumption of her yoke upon his passions, seemed to her only his due chastisement; every pang which she detected in him, every look of remorse, every imprudence of utterance or regard, pleased her as witness of his just degradation. In the many occasions which society gave her, she planted daggers in his breast with every cruelly chosen word she spoke, which was invariably veiled in easy irony or simulated friendliness, until his whole existence was consumed between the longing for, and the dread of, her approach. She had towards him a mingling of compassion, raillery, and kindness, which was of all means the one most certain to wound, excite, and enchain him. Whenever he was within hearing, she was in her wittiest moods, her most brilliant aspects; all the various charms of her acute intelligence and of her high culture seemed increased tenfold after the simple childlike speech and the convent-bred mind of his young wife. He felt like a man who, long chained to a narrow, colourless, peaceful shore, is suddenly set free amidst the flowering labyrinths and the voluptuous odours of a tropical savannah.

Never had Nadine Napraxine been so willing to please, so facile to be pleased, as in the course of this Paris winter, when he was constantly within sight of her coquetteries, within earshot of her speeches. He watched her across a salon as a captive sunk in the depths of a prison may gaze at a summer sky beneath which he may never again stand a free man. The sense of his vicinity and of his suffering, supplied that stimulant to life which her languid emotions needed; she viewed the drama of his regret and revolt with an interest in it half bitter, half sweet. A man who could have wedded another whilst he loved herself, deserved, she told herself, to suffer; yet there were moments when, beneath her triumphs and her mockeries, there was in her own heart a thrill of answering pain; what might have been, glided also before her memory with pale reproach.

One night, entirely by chance, he and she were alone for a few minutes, that solitude in a crowd for which great entertainments give so much opportunity.

It was at a ball given by Prince Orloff; those hazards of society which it always amused her to subdue and turn to the service of her own intentions, had brought him to her side; some great palms made a little grove around them; the sound of the valse from Faust came dreamily from the distant ball-room.

'Do you know, Othmar, that I am disappointed in you?' she murmured, in her softest, cruellest, most malicious tones. 'I imagined that you would be so very good to your wife; you were always sighing to be an *homme d'intérieur*, you were always coveting solitude, sentiment, and sympathy. I expected to see you give us the example of a perfectly ideal union; but I am afraid that, after all, you are not much better than other men.'

'Madame——'

'Oh, you are angry, of course! Everyone is angry who is in the wrong. It is perfectly true, you are only a husband like ten thousand others. You were always a little like Chateaubriand: "Touriste, ambassadeur, ministre, ou amant, à peine arrivé, il s'ennuie."'

'It might be true of M. de Chateaubriand,' said Othmar, with displeasure, 'it is not so of me. I am most constant,—where I have never been welcome.'

The confession escaped him despite himself, and he regretted it passionately as soon as it was uttered.

'That is why you are faithful,' said Nadine Napraxine, smiling. 'If you had been welcome, how poor and pale the whole country of your explorations would have seemed to you! There is only one way not to have shut on you those dreadful gates of disillusion; it is to be wise, and never to pass through them.'

'Your philosophies are, no doubt, madame, as correct as your observations,' said Othmar, with impatience.

'I pass my life in observing,' she replied. 'It is the only pursuit in society which has really any interest in it. But tell me, do you not a little, just a little, neglect your wife? It is a pity, she is so young; in time, if you be not there, someone else will be.'

'Never!' he interrupted, with some heat. 'I have many faults, no doubt, and I abandon them to your observation; but Yseulte has not a single defect that I have seen; she is loyalty, innocence, and honour incarnated.'

'They are three charming qualities,' replied Nadine Napraxine, 'but they do not appear to have any result except that of making you dangerously confident that you may leave them wholly to themselves.'

Othmar coloured; he was sensible of the correctness of the accusation, and it irritated him excessively to hear the woman he loved rebuke him for his conduct to his wife.

'If I be too indifferent where all my allegiance should be given,' he said abruptly, 'the Princess Napraxine should be the last on earth to accuse me of it. She knows the cause.'

'The cause, I imagine, is in your temperament,' she replied, ignoring his meaning, 'as it was in Chateaubriand's.'

'Can we not leave Chateaubriand alone?'

'And speak only of yourself? It is a curious thing, but a man is never contented unless he is speaking solely of himself. It is the only entity in which he takes any real interest.'

'Perhaps it is the only one with which he is really conversant.'

'Oh, you must be conversant with your wife's. Her mind must be as clear as crystal. Do you know, Othmar, I think you ought to be more grateful than you are; to have so very pure a creature as that to be the mother of your children, is a privilege to you and to your race.'

She spoke gravely for the moment, abandoning the ironical mockery of her habitual tone.

He rose abruptly.

'I cannot be grateful,' he said very low, with a passionate vibration in his voice. 'I was a fool, and I committed a great error. With all my life burnt up by one love, I imagined that I could slake the flames of it by contact with youth and innocence, as if the woodland brook could cool and arrest the boiling lava!'

Nadine Napraxine heard, with her languid lids drooped over her eyes, and the shadow of a smile upon her mouth.

'If it were so, you should be too proud to confess it,' she said, after a pause. 'To be sure it is not a very confidential confession, for everyone sees that your—experiment—has not been quite so successful as you hoped, as Baron Fritz, at least, hoped. Well, we have talked long enough in this solitude; you may take me to the ball-room.'

When he went home, no sleep came to him that night; his conscience and his pride rebuked him for the admission he had made, and before his eyes there passed ceaselessly the vision of Nadine Napraxine, pale, ethereal, magically seductive, like those figures of Herculaneum which float noiselessly in the air, their bodies delicate as the gossamer-winged body of the Deilephila.

And she had said to him, 'All the world sees that your experiment has not succeeded!'

The words added the one drop of mortification and of bitterness which was alone wanting in the cup which he had of his own weakness and of his own will filled for himself, and was forced by the justice of fate to drink.

She herself drove homeward alone through the chilly shadows of the dawn, which could not touch her, wrapped in her eider-down lined satins, and reclining amongst her yielding cushions. A beggar woman sitting on a doorstep with a sick child sleepless in her arms, saw the carriage pass, and thought, 'What must it feel like to roll on like that, clad like that, warm and happy like that, with the price of a million loaves of bread in one single stone at your throat?'

Nadine Napraxine would have told her that food and warmth and jewels were no especial pleasure, when you had been always used to them; perhaps the absence of them might be painful—so much she would have granted.

She drove homeward, and went up to her white dressing-room with a vague sense of impatience and of regret stirring within her.

How he loved her, how he loved her, although he had been madman enough to give his life to another in an insane attempt to attain oblivion!

She did not lie down, but when her women had undressed her and wrapped her in her loose warm wrappers, she sat long looking dreamily into the fire burning on the open hearth, for the night of April was chilly within doors though without nightingales began to sing amidst the lilac buds. He would still, if she chose, go far away from all duty, all honour, all the ways of the world and the respect of men. Almost it tempted her, that which she had rejected two years before. There was another life to be hurt now! Friederich Othmar had perchance read her temperament aright when he had thought that the power to make misery would have greater force to attract her than the power to confer happiness.

'I suppose I must be what the good dullards call wicked,' she thought with a smile at herself, and a certain vague emotion of disgust at her own impulse.

Was she wicked? Was anybody so? Was there ever anything in human nature beyond impatience, ennui, inquisitiveness, natural love of dominion, and wholly instinctive egotism? Did not these, collectively or singly, suffice to account for all human actions?

CHAPTER XLIII.

A few days later Nadine Napraxine was surprised and annoyed at receiving in the forenoon a request from her husband that she would be so good as to receive him for a few moments.

'Beg the Prince to excuse me,' she said to her women. 'I am tired and must go out in an hour.'

Never once in the years of their marriage had Napraxine ever ventured to insist after such a message, or to revolt against her decisions. She was astonished and exceedingly irritated when they brought her a pencilled note in which were written some blurred words: 'Pray pardon me, but I have urgent reasons to desire to see you without delay; I must entreat of you to admit me, if only for a moment.'

'*Quelle corvée!*' she murmured as she reluctantly gave the order to let him enter. The companionship of her husband, at all times wearisome to her, had become in the last few weeks more than usually intolerable.

'I must beg of you not to send me these autocratic demands,' she said, with much impatience, as he entered. 'You want my women sent away? Why should they be sent away? What can you possibly have to say that may not be heard from the housetops?'

Looking at him with irritation and undisguised dislike, she saw an expression upon his face which was new there; he motioned the maids away with authority; he was disturbed and excited; he had nevertheless a certain dignity and anger in his attitude.

'Do you know, madame,' he said abruptly when they were alone, being scarcely conscious of what he did say, 'that here in Paris there are persons who venture to hint that—that—that Othmar has been for many years at your feet? That his marriage was only one of pique? That even now he neglects his wife because of you? Had you any idea of this? Can you tell me what possible foundation there is for it? Oh, do not think for a moment that I pay any heed to it, only I would like to know why—when——'

Entangled in his words and in his ideas, he stammered, breathed heavily, came to a full pause; he dared not accuse her, did not even accuse her in his own thoughts; but the sudden knowledge that her name was spoken in union with Othmar's had so galled and stunned him that he had lost his usual patience, his habitual timidity, before her.

His wife heard him with a contraction of her eyebrows, which was the only sign she ever gave of anger; her eyes were cold and haughty; her whole countenance was as unrevealing as the marble features of her bust by Dupré which stood on a table near. For the sole time in her life she was not prepared with a reply; the various memories which had united herself and Othmar had been always so carefully veiled from the knowledge of others that she had never imagined any outer light would be ever shed upon them. The world had certainly seen at one time that Othmar loved her, and had been ready to sacrifice his life at her word, but that had been long ago; she had not supposed that the emotions which her clairvoyance had discovered, the mesmerism which she still exercised, had had any spectators. But if for the moment surprised, she was never for a moment at fault. She looked steadily at her husband, with the delicate lines of her eyebrows drawn together in a frown, which lent a strange severity to her features.

'My dear Prince,' she said slowly and coldly; 'you have known my character for nearly eight years. I cannot tell whether the opportunities you have had of understanding it have been employed to the utmost, or whether your powers of comprehension have been not altogether equal to the task. But one thing at least I should have supposed you would have learned in all that time—I should have thought you would have understood that I do not permit impertinent interrogation, or even interrogation at all. I never ask you questions; I expect never to be asked them.'

Napraxine stood before her like a chidden child; his long habit of deference to her will and fear of her superiority were still in the ascendant with him, but struggling against them were his own manliness, and a vague, new-born suspicion, strengthened by a certain evasiveness, which even his sluggish intelligence perceived, in her reply.

'After all,' he said, somewhat piteously and irrelevantly; 'after all, Nadège, I am your husband.'

'Unhappily!'

The single word so chill and so contemptuous was cast at him like a blow with crystals of ice. He shrank a little.

'No doubt you think so, though I have done what I could,' he said, humbly repressing the pang he felt. 'But unhappily or not, the fact is a fact. You permit me very few conjugal rights, but there is one which you will not surely deny me—the right to know what truth or untruth there is in these stories of Othmar?'

'You speak like a *juge d'instruction!*' she said, with all her customary disdain. 'You ought to let no one tell you those or any other stories. It is yourself whom they make ridiculous, not me.'

'No one shall make me so long,' he muttered. 'If you will not answer me, I will go to him.'

She raised her head haughtily and looked him full in the face with that gaze wherewith she was accustomed to cow and to coerce men as the shepherd's voice intimidates and rules the sheep.

'That would be certainly original,' she said, with a slight suggestion of laughter. 'A husband going to an imaginary lover to beg him to reveal how high he stood in the favour of his wife!—it would be original if it would not be dignified. I wonder what Othmar would answer you! You will admit that it would be a great temptation to his vanity—and his invention!'

Napraxine paced a few steps to and fro the room in an agitation which every one of her languid and contemptuous words increased; a kind of hopelessness always came over him in the presence of his wife; it was so impossible to move, to touch, to hold, to comprehend her. The calm raillery, the chill imperious anger, which were all he ever could excite in her, left his heart so shrunken and wounded, his pride so humiliated and baffled.

He paused before her suddenly.

'Nadège,' he said, with a tremor in his voice: 'You know that I have always liked Othmar. You asked me once why. It is not much of a narrative. This is it. One day, years and years ago, when he was quite a youth, we chanced to travel together in Russia. There was a movement of agrarian revolt at that time. As we passed a village in the province of Moscow we came upon a horrible conflagration; there were incendiary fires; great sheepfolds and cattle-pens were burning. I—Heaven forgive my selfishness!—would have driven on; I only wanted to get to Moscow itself in time for a masked ball at the Kremlin; but Othmar would not; he sprang out of the carriage and rallied a few men around him, and plunged right into the flames to save the sheep and the cattle, or such of them as he could; of course when he did that, I had no choice but to do the same. We worked all night; we saved thousands of the beasts, but we lost the ball at the Kremlin. I do not say it was anything very great to do. I dare say numbers of other young men would have done as much; but the remembrance of it has always made me like Othmar. If you had seen him scorched, and singed, and black with smoke, his hair burnt and his hands blistered, dragging the rams and the ewes, driving the bullocks and heifers, the flames curling up over the grass which was as dry as chips, for it was in the month of August;—I have always liked him ever since; he is not the mere ennuyé that they think him.'

He paused abruptly; his wife's eyes had a conflicting expression in them; there was emotion and there was mockery.

'Oh fool!—oh poor big innocent fool!' she thought, '*you* to praise Otho Othmar to me!'

Yet something in what he had said softened her cynical intolerance of his questions and made her more merciful to him. The only qualities which were ever admirable to her in her husband were his courage and his sympathy with courage. They were not uncommon attributes, but they were those which always had affinity to hers. And the half-grotesque, half-pathetic ignorance which was visible as he spoke of Othmar moved her to a certain indulgence in all her scorn.

'He is so stupid, but he is so honest,' she thought, as she had thought so often before, with a feeling of compassion which might in any other woman have been a pang of conscience. However, the passing sentiment could not altogether exclude her more dominant instincts of raillery, her not easily appeased offence at interrogation and interference.

'I do not really see, my dear Napraxine,' she said languidly, 'what possible connection singed sheep and burning heifers have to do with the rumours which—you say—society has been so good as to set on foot concerning me. It is unfortunate that your ideas are always so entangled that it is very difficult to follow them. But I imagine, so far as I can evolve anything from such a chaos, that what you intend me to understand by all this is, that because one summer night in Russia long ago you were witness of a courageous action on the part of—your friend—you would be sorry to suppose that he would commit one which would make him your enemy: is that so?'

Napraxine made a gesture of assent.

'I cannot express myself well,' he murmured. 'But you are so clever you can always understand——'

'To sort the black and the white beans set to Psyche for a task were easier,' quoted his wife, with her enigmatical smile. 'Still, if I interpret your meaning aright, it is that. Pray, then, let your mind be at rest; the Countess Othmar is not neglected that I know of, and if she be, *je n'y suis pour rien.*'

Then she poured out her chocolate. Napraxine was reassured by her indifferent manner, and did not observe that the major part of his interrogations was still left unanswered.

'I was sure of it,' he said with warmth. 'He is very much in love with her, is he not?'

She gave a slight, most eloquent gesture, indicative of absolute ignorance and of as absolute indifference.

'Ah! that is another matter which I could not presume to decide,' she answered with a little yawn. 'He has been married fourteen months; men are not usually in love so long as that.'

'I——' began Napraxine: then he stammered, paused, and coloured, afraid of her ridicule.

'Yes; you were,' said his wife, serenely. 'But it is very unusual; it is very undesirable. I do not think it contributed to your comfort; it certainly did not to mine.'

Napraxine sighed.

'I should have never changed,' he said with ardour, though with timidity, as though he were a lover of eighteen.

'You have never changed,' she said with that smile which she could render enchanting in sweetness and in graciousness. 'You have always been much better to me than I have deserved, and you have always been the most generous and the most amiable of men. Now go; I have many things to do, and I want my women.'

Napraxine grew red with pleasure at her praise, and his pale eyes shone with eagerness, delight, and the admiration which she had hated so intensely in the early years of their marriage. He stooped towards her, breathless with his gratitude, and his hopes suddenly aroused after so many years of despair and of resignation.

'Nadine,' he murmured. 'Even now—now—if you would? None of them have loved you as I do.'

She stretched out her hand so that his lips, which would fain have gone elsewhere, were forced to remain there.

'Perhaps,' she said vaguely, still with that enchanting smile which was to him like a glimpse into Paradise itself. 'Do not ask for too much at first; *au revoir.*'

Then she rang for her maids, and he was forced to withdraw; but he went with all the forces of a re-awakened passion throbbing in his veins and beating at his heart, like a swarm of bees roused by a ray of warmth from winter torpor.

She, as soon as his step had ceased to echo along the distant corridors, and the sound of wheels and horses' feet in the courtyard below told her that he was about to leave the house, dismissed her women, saying that she wished to sleep, and sat alone, with a sense of strong disgust and of vague anxiety upon her.

'I could not allow him to provoke Othmar,' she thought. 'Anything but that! anything but that!'

She would have been capable of any self-sacrifice, of any concession to her husband, which could have prevented the hostile meeting of those men.

A sudden tide of strong emotion swept over her self-centred and languid life. In that one moment, in which she had become conscious of a possible danger to Othmar, she had become as conscious of the full force of her regard for him. Love, which had been her victim, her plaything, her instrument, her servitor, for so long, became at length the guest of her own heart, and was stronger than herself. She had driven that danger away from his path by the skill of her consummate finesse; but she was not wholly reassured, and if to save him from her husband's suspicions she would be compelled to make herself the recipient of her husband's re-awakened tenderness, she felt that the price would be more hateful than death.

Even the momentary constraint and feigning which she had put upon herself with her husband stung all her pride, offended all her dignity; she could take no delight in it as she did usually in the admirable issues of her most admirable skill in seduction and dissimulation. A certain impression, which was not profound enough to be shame but had its character, remained with her. She had been successful as usual, but success did not content her. She was exceedingly proud; her delicacy, which was as susceptible as any sensitive plant to any rude approach, shrank from the path into which she had entered. She could take an intellectual pleasure in adroit dissimulation, but she had no pleasure in deceiving an honest confidence. She had always despised with all the scorn of her nature the covered ways of intrigue, the hidden resorts of illicit desires; her taste as well as her pride had always preserved her from the pitfalls to which other women danced with light hearts and light steps. Some sense of approaching these perils touched her now and offended her, as with the presence of some vulgar thing. She saw clearly enough what Othmar perhaps did not or would not see, that their mutual love would soon or late take them on that same road which all lovers have taken since the days when the Book was read beneath the garden trees of Rimini. She was not alarmed or troubled in any moral sense, but her delicacy and her hauteur were disturbed. For the first time, she felt that it was possible for events and sentiments to have more control over her than she had over them; for the first time she had the sensation of being drawn on by fate in lieu of herself controlling it.

CHAPTER XLIV.

In the excitation of his new hopes and of his happy self-delusions her husband's suspicions had all died away; he did not even notice how completely she had avoided all direct answer to the questions which had at the first so offended her. He had not the faintest conception of how completely he had been put off his guard, intoxicated by suggested concessions, and enwrapped in the blinding fumes of awakening affections.

He went, with his usual heavy and slow tread, but with a heart as light as a youth's who has heard the first word of encouragement from lips he loved, out into the noon-day glare of the Paris streets. During these six years through which his wife had been no more to him than the tea-rose which she liked to wear at her throat, he had grown reconciled to the inevitable. He had consoled himself with the thousand and one consolations with which women are always ready to strew the path of a rich man; he had not, after the first shock of her dislike, greatly rebelled or greatly mourned; and he had been what his world called a *viveur enragé*. Yet at the depths of his soul there had been always—living, tenacious, indestructible, exceedingly humble, and infinitely forgiving—a great love for his wife. If she had cared, she could have done what she chose with him; he would have led the life of an anchorite to win her favour, and there would have been no heroism and no folly to which she could not have impelled him. She had never seen in him anything except a heavy, stupid, good-humoured man, who could have a very good manner when it was wanted, but had hardly more intelligence than one of his own *moujiks*. She never saw the possibilities of self-negation and of blind devotion which slumbered in his nature because she never felt interest enough in him to look for them. To see as little of him as was possible, whilst still remaining in accordance with the etiquette of the world, was all her study where Platon Napraxine was concerned.

That he loved her very much she was fully aware—loved her as only big dogs and unintellectual people have the instinct to do—but the higher qualities which were in him, and might have been called out had she chosen, she never knew or would have cared to know. The natural nobility of his character was entirely obscured to her beneath the slowness and dulness of his intelligence, as his corpulent body and his large appetite wholly concealed the heroism of poor Louis Seize from France and from the world.

Napraxine, when he left her now, walked straight to a private club which he often frequented; a club of great exclusiveness and distinction, where very high play could be indulged in every morning, afternoon, and evening. There he breakfasted, played a little himself to while away time, and waited the coming of the Duc de Prangins. He waited until four o'clock; at that hour, which was his usual one for entrance there, the elder de Prangins arrived for his customary afternoon baccarat.

Napraxine threw down the cards he held, rose, and approached him.

'M. le Duc,' he said curtly, 'I have learned that you have ventured to jest about Madame la Princesse Napraxine. I am here to tell you that I do not allow such jests. If you apologise for them—well. If not——'

'I never apologise,' said the Duc, as curtly.

Napraxine, without more words, struck him over the shoulders with a cane which he carried. Then he turned his back on him with supreme disdain, and sat down again to his écarté.

To such an insult there was only one answer possible. Within fifteen minutes a hostile meeting was arranged between him and M. de Prangins, which was to take place on the following morning at sunrise, in the gardens of a friend's château situated on the road to Versailles.

The elder de Prangins, though a man of sixty-five years of age, was of great skill and address in all offensive and defensive science; it was he who had killed the young Piedmontese prince, d'Ivrea, some four years before. He was a slightly-made man, but very strong and agile, cold and sure in his attack, and very careful in his guard. He had the reputation of being a dangerous foe, and, secure in that reputation, had never condescended to bridle his tongue, which was at once coarse and caustic. For Nadine Napraxine he had conceived, years earlier, one of those gross, yet chill, passions of which a man, advanced in years, is at once tenacious and impatient, proud and ashamed.

Platon Napraxine finished his game of écarté and won it. He was in no degree disturbed or depressed by the ordeal which lay before him. He was as happy as a boy to think that he was about to fight in her cause, and he pictured to himself how, when all was over, he would tell her, and perhaps—perhaps—she would smile on him for the recital. Like many big, strong, and kindly men, he had a great deal of the lad in him; he was unworn in heart, despite all the experiences of his life in Paris and in Petersburg; the adoration of his wife, which he had preserved throughout all the vulgar amours with which he had sought to console himself, had served, in a great measure, to keep his youth alive in him. With a youth's hopefulness and short-sightedness he longed now for the moment in which he would say to her, 'They dared to jest of you, but I was there; and they have bitten the dust.'

That night she dined at one house and he dined at another; she went later to more than one ball, at which she showed herself for a brief hour of the cotillon and then took herself away, knowing that after her presence there all other women would pale and pall, as the stars fade, or seem to fade, when a meteor passes. She and Othmar had met that night at more than one house, and she had kept him beside her more openly and for a longer time than she had ever done before. It was her manner of reply to her husband's suspicions and to the conjectures of the world.

Platon Napraxine returned home earlier than usual, and waited in a little smoking-room which opened on to the head of the staircase that he might hear her arrival, and see her once, if only as she passed up the stairs. It was only midnight when he went home, and he waited one, two, three, four hours; then he heard the carriage roll into the inner court and the door of the private entrance open. He left the *fumoir* and walked a few steps downward to meet her as she ascended the staircase. His heart thrilled as he saw her in her cloak, made of soft blush-coloured feathers, with her delicate head emerging from it as from some rose-tinted cloud. She herself perceived him waiting there with that involuntary irresistible sense of annoyance which was always her first emotion whenever she saw him anywhere.

She gave him a little careless smile, nodded a good-night, and would have gone onward, but he stopped her timidly.

'Give me one of those,' he said, as he touched the knot of tea-roses which were fastened at her breast.

'What nonsense!' she said impatiently, with much real irritation, as she mused, 'If he play the lover, I shall not keep my patience!'

Her cloak parted and fell a little off one arm. His eyes dwelled passionately on the whiteness of her shoulder, with the great diamonds sparkling on it, and the jewelled butterflies trembling as though they took the blue veins for azure flowers.

With an obstinacy which he had never dared to show to her before he drew away one of the tea-roses.

'Do not be angry,' he murmured.

She shrugged her shoulders with sovereign indifference and contempt, and passed up the stairs.

He looked after her with dim longing eyes.

No shadow of any sort had been upon him throughout that sunny day— the last day of April.

The next morning he went with a perfectly light heart to the garden outside Paris which had been chosen as the scene of his encounter with the Duc de Prangins. He had fought many duels in his time; he was a fine fencer, though of late he had neglected to keep his hand in practice, and he was a man always of the coolest and most stolid courage. He had no kind of apprehension of the result; he had taken no measures in case he should fall; it seemed so entirely impossible; besides, all his affairs were in order, all his vast wealth was disposed of with legal accuracy and care in documents which were safe in their iron safes in the muniment room of Zaraizoff; he went to his appointment with no more thought or apprehension than he would have gone to the 'tir aux pigeons.'

He lighted a large cigar and stood chatting with his friends to the last moment. Now and then he put his hand in his coat; it was to feel for the little rose he had taken from her the day before; but his friends could not know that.

For some moments after the rapiers crossed the duel was bloodless; a mere display of even and perfect science on each side; but at the third encounter his guard was broken; the sword of the Duc de Prangins entered his left side and passed straight through the left lung out beneath the shoulder; his adversary could not draw it back; with the blade transfixing his breast thus, Platon Napraxine fell heavily to the ground. When they endeavoured to raise him he looked at them, and his lips moved; it was only the hoarsest murmur, but it said once, twice, thrice—'Do not tell her! Do not tell her! Do not tell her!'

They let him lie where he was; they gathered about him pale and in silence. They all knew he was a dead man.

For one moment he looked up at the blue morning sky where the clouds were drifting and a flock of swallows was circling with gay buoyant movement; there were all the odours of spring on the air, and the grass which he lay on was yellow with kingcups and white with daisies. With his right hand he feebly made the sign of the cross on his breast; then he thrust the same hand within his coat once more, and with a terrible shuddering, choking sigh his last breath passed away. When they unloosened his lifeless fingers they found them clasped on a faded tea-rose.

'Who will tell Princess Napraxine?' said the men around him, with white lips, to one another.

The man who had killed him, throwing on his great-coat in haste, said with a cruel smile:

'She will have a Te Deum in every church in Paris. You waste your pity.'

CHAPTER XLV.

Nadine Napraxine had just quitted her bathroom, and was taking her chocolate, when her women, vaguely frightened and so venturing to disobey her, brought her word that Prince Ezarhédine begged to see her for a few moments on an urgent matter. It was noon. She was never visible until three in the daytime in Paris. She was at first indignant at such an insolence, then made curious by such an intrusion. Ezarhédine had been one of her husband's familiar associates, but he had never been an intimate friend of her own.

'What can he want?' she said irritably. 'Send M. Valisoff to him.'

Valisoff was her own secretary.

But when her servants insisted, contrary to all their usual timid obedience to her rules, her inquisitiveness was excited; she consented to receive the unbidden and ill-timed visit. She cast about her a loose gown of cream-hued China crape, embroidered with pansies and primroses, put her feet into slippers which were embroidered like it, and with her beautiful arms seen through the loose sleeves, and her eyes still suffused with the languor of her morning sleep, she passed out into the small salon adjoining her dressing-chamber.

Prince Ezarhédine, ushered in there, bowed to the ground, and then stood looking at her strangely. He was very pale, and there was a tremor about his mouth.

'Madame,' he murmured, and then paused; his voice could not be commanded.

She, with her wonderful and instantaneous penetration into the minds of those who spoke to her, divined his mission in that one moment in which his eyes met hers. She went a step nearer to him, herself looking like some Aurora of the Italian painters, with her white floating flower-embroidered robes and her loose hair bound by an amethyst-hued ribbon.

'What have you come to tell me?' she said, in a strange, low voice. 'Is my husband—dead?'

Ezarhédine bowed in silence.

She shuddered slightly from head to foot; her eyes opened wide with an expression of great terror; her lips turned white. She sat down on the nearest seat, and motioned to him to be seated by her.

'Has he fought with Othmar?' she said hoarsely, so low that her words were scarcely intelligible.

'With Othmar? No, madame,' Ezarhédine answered in surprise; and told her with whom he had fought and how he had died.

She heard in perfect silence; but the colour had returned to her lips.

'Poor Napraxine; he died for her sake, and it is only of Othmar that she thought,' mused Prince Ezarhédine as he left her house when his painful mission was over.

CHAPTER XLVI.

Othmar was in his own house that day at two o'clock looking at a portrait, by Cabanel, of his wife, which had been sent home in the forenoon, and which had been left standing in the salon, where she passed most of her hours. The portrait was one of the triumphs of that elegant master. He had painted her in a gown of white velvet, with her favourite peacocks near, and some high shrubs of red azaleas to lend her the contrast of rich colour. The whole composition was a masterpiece of softness, brilliancy, and sunshine. Othmar stood looking at it and speaking of it to the Baron and to Yseulte when Alain de Vannes was ushered into the room, and, scarcely pausing for the usual ceremonies of salutation, said abruptly to him: 'You have heard the news of the morning? Napraxine is dead.'

The Duc had calculated the effect of his abrupt speech. Othmar, on whose features the full light was falling from a window of which the curtains had been drawn back for the examination of Cabanel's portrait, changed colour violently, and his whole face expressed the force of conflicting emotions with which he was moved. Yseulte watched him, fascinated with a vague terror; she had never seen him violently moved under the influence of any strong feeling.

Friederich Othmar, alone retaining his calmness, answered in amazement: 'Napraxine! Napraxine dead! Are you certain? I saw him last night at midnight; he was in full health and spirits.'

'Nevertheless he is dead,' said De Vannes, keeping his gaze on Othmar; and he related the circumstances of the duel.

Othmar listened in profound silence; he had recovered his self-control, but the colour had not returned to his face.

'What was the cause?' asked Friederich Othmar, when he had heard all that there was to hear.

Alain de Vannes shrugged his shoulders.

'De Prangins had spoken jestingly of the Princess—and someone else. Napraxine heard of it through some lamentable indiscretion; he insulted the old Duke; and the result is what I have said. He was run through the lungs and died in a few moments. De Prangins relieved Madame Napraxine of a troublesome lad in young d'Ivrea; he has now done her a still greater service by ridding her of the only ennui in her life which she was sometimes compelled to endure. I do not know who told her what had happened, but the body of Napraxine has already been taken to his house. The duel was fought in a private garden at Versailles.'

Then he paused, having no more to say, and, like a good orator, being unwilling to destroy by detail and diffuseness the effect of his unexpected statement.

Othmar muttered a few sentences of conventional regret and turned away to where the picture stood. Yseulte followed him with wistful eyes. She felt that the news had shocked and startled him strangely, but she was afraid to seem to have remarked his agitation. After a few moments he made some trivial excuse, and left the room.

Friederich Othmar resumed his occupation of examining Cabanel's work through a lorgnon: people whom he knew died every day; it was not such a simple event as that which could cause him any excitement, and Platon Napraxine, though a very great person in his own way, had no place in the public life of Europe.

The Duc de Vannes approached Yseulte.

'My cousin,' he said with gentle mockery, 'was poor Napraxine such a favourite of yours that you look so stricken with sorrow? If I had known that my intelligence would have caused such regret, I would have been less precipitate in relating it.'

Yseulte coloured; she was conscious that it was her husband's emotion, not hers, at which he jested.

'Death is always terrible,' she murmured, not knowing what to say. 'And Prince Napraxine always seemed so well, so strong, so full of health——'

De Vannes laughed a little grimly.

'Poor Napraxine had only one vulnerable point—his heart; some gossiper pecked at that as jays peck at fruit; and this is the end. You know he adored his wife, most unfortunately for himself; she is called the Marie Stuart of our day, and to complete the parallel, it was necessary for her to be the cause of her husband's death.'

'But—she must suffer now?' said Yseulte, her golden eyes dim and dark with feeling.

'Suffer?' echoed Alain de Vannes. 'I see you do not know Madame Napraxine, though you meet so often. The long strict Russian mourning and all the religious rites will weary her terribly. Beyond that, she will not be much distressed, and she will have many—consolations.'

'She has children,' said Yseulte.

The Duc smiled.

'It was not of her children that I was thinking,' he said with meaning.

Friederich Othmar turned round from his examination of the portrait.

'My child,' he said to Yseulte, 'will you pardon me if I remind you that your horses have been waiting a long time, and that the *matinée* at Princess Hohenlohe's will be more than half over. M. le Duc will be kind enough to excuse the hint; he is always so amiable.'

Yseulte, who was still obedient with the unquestioning submission of her childish days, rose and bade adieu to her cousin, then went to her own apartments.

Friederich Othmar turned to the Duke:

'Shall we walk down the boulevard together?' he suggested, whilst he thought to himself, 'That fox shall not get at her ear if I can help it.'

While Alain de Vannes assented and they sauntered down the staircase of Othmar's house, the Duc said with a pleasant little laugh:

'Ah, my dear Baron, if this duel had taken place with the same results fifteen months ago my little cousin would not have been mistress here!'

'Who knows?' said Friederich Othmar, vaguely, with that bland indifference which was his favourite mask and weapon.

CHAPTER XLVII.

As Yseulte went to her own room her way led her past the great cedar-wood doors of her husband's library, that retreat where he passed so many of those hours of meditation and of pain,—such hours as in old days led men of his nature to the isolation of the cloister. He had always told her that she was free to enter there; but the delicacy of her temper had always made her use the privilege but rarely; so rarely, that he had ceased ever to be afraid of her entrance in moments when the lassitude or the dejection of his life overcame him and made him little willing to meet her gaze. Now, as she passed by the door, a wistful impulse moved her to see him, to speak to him, to be spoken to by him. She had an instinctive feeling that this news of Napraxine's death had caused him a greater shock than she could comprehend or measure; all the affection, the adoration, which she bore him went out to him in this incomprehensible sorrow.

'If he would only tell me'—she thought.

Inspired by that longing for his confidence, she opened the door. Othmar sat at his writing-table, and his head was bowed down on his arms; his back was to her, but his whole attitude expressed extreme weariness, exceeding sorrow. When he sprang to his feet at the sound of the opening door, she saw that his eyes were wet with tears. He suppressed both his emotion and his irritation as best he could, and said to her gently:

'Do you want me, my dear? Wait a moment; I will be with you.'

He turned from her as if to sort some papers on his table. She did not advance; she stood looking at him with a scared, colourless face: a truth had come into her mind swift and venomous as an adder. She thought suddenly:

'If I were not here—she could be his wife—now.'

The secret of his uncontrollable emotion at the tidings of Napraxine's death was laid bare to her in one of those flashes of thought which light up the brain as lightning illumines the landscape. She murmured some vague words and left the room: her long training in silence and self-suppression gave her strength to repress the cry which rose to her lips.

Othmar scarcely heeded her departure or heard her answer: his own pain and restless rebellion against the fate which he had made for himself absorbed him.

'Poor innocent child!' he thought once with self-reproach. 'She must never know; it was I who sought her—I must keep her in her illusions as best I may.'

He did not know that her illusions had been killed in that moment of cruel certainty, as once in the church of S. Pharamond his orchids and azaleas had perished in a single night of frost.

She told her people to have the horses taken back to the stables: she felt unwell; she would not go out that morning; then she locked herself in her own apartments. She could not face that world of Paris, which would be speaking all the day of one theme,—the death of Prince Napraxine.

It was the last day of April; the sunshine was streaming through the gardens of the great hotel, and through her open windows there came the scent of opening lilac buds and blossoming hawthorn boughs. Like the year and the earth, she was in the early sweetness of her youth; yet old age hardly knows a more chill and cruel sense of loneliness and desolation than was with her now as she lay, face downward, on her bed, and sobbed her youth away. With instantaneous and merciless force the truth had broken in upon her at last; she suddenly realised that she had no place in the heart of Othmar, and was but a burden on his life. She realised that she had been taken in pity, wedded in generosity and compassion, but without one passing gleam or throb of love. She marvelled that she could have been so blind before. All the memories which thronged upon her brought with them a thousand inexorable witnesses of the truth. The knowledge of the world which she had learned of late was like a lamp shedding its cruel rays on every damning fact.

For long she had known, she had felt, that her husband cared only for one woman upon earth, and that woman not herself. But never until now had the conviction come to her of how cruelly and eternally she barred the way between him and his happiness and his desires. The weakness and the defects of the early training which she had received now told upon her character, making her shut close in her own soul all she suffered, and enabling her to keep perfect silence on all she had discovered. Without that acquired habit of reserve, her natural candour and trustfulness would have impelled her to give some confidence, to receive some counsel, in her dire distress, would have even brought her to her husband's side. But the pride which was in her blood was united with the power of self-repression engendered by the teachings she had received. In any sorrow which had not also been humiliation, in any fault which had been her own, not his, she would have thrown herself at Othmar's feet and confessed all that she felt. But this was impossible to her now; the words would have choked her; she could not say to him: 'I know I am only a pensioner on your pity and your generosity;' she could not say to him, 'I know that I stand between you and one whom you loved before ever you saw me.' More undisciplined and less delicate tempers might have found some refuge in such passionate lamentation and revelation, but to Yseulte de Valogne such outbursts of reproach were impossible; they would have been contrary to every habit of her young life, to every tradition of the order and of the race from which she sprang. 'The vulgar cry out when they are hurt,' her grandmother had said once to her during the siege of Paris; 'but for us—there are only two things possible—either vengeance or silence.'

Those words came back upon her mind as she lay upon her bed, whilst the sweet fresh winds of the spring-time blew the scent of the lilac and hawthorn across her chamber. Vengeance there could be none for her; he had been her saviour, her protector, her kindest friend, her lover, whom she adored with all the ignorant, innocent, mute worship of first love; there only remained the alternative—silence.

There was something of the dumb obstinacy of the Breton in her, and much also of the Breton force of heroism; the heroism which does not speak, but bears and acts, immovable and uncomplaining. That great strength of endurance enabled her now to recover her self-control by the time that she was forced to meet Othmar again, and to go into her drawing-rooms at eight o'clock before the hour of dinner, with no trace of what she had suffered upon her except in the pallor of her face and the dark shade beneath her eyes.

'Are you feeling ill, my dear child?' said her husband, as he met her. 'I hear you have not been out to-day, and you had many engagements?'

She murmured some vague answer;—she had been lying down; her head ached.

He answered her with some tender expressions of regret, and inquired no more. Her health was delicate and fluctuating at that moment; he supposed that it was natural that she had such occasional hours of depression.

They chanced to be alone at dinner that evening, which was unusual. Neither of them spoke many words. When he addressed her it was with the utmost kindliness and gentleness of tone, but he said little, and his own preoccupation prevented him from noticing how constrained were her replies, how forced her smiles.

She observed, with a cruel tightening of her heart, that he never alluded to the death of his friend Napraxine.

When dinner was over, she said to him very calmly:

'There are several engagements for tonight too, but if you will allow me, I will stay at home. I am a little—tired.'

'Certainly, my dear,' he said at once. 'Never go into the world but when it amuses you; and your health is of far more value than any other consideration. Shall I call your physicians?'

'Oh no; it is nothing. I am only a little fatigued,' she said hurriedly; and as he stooped to touch her cheek with his lips she turned her head quickly, and for the first time avoided his caress.

He was too absorbed in his own thoughts even to observe the significance of the involuntary gesture. He led her to the doors of her own apartments, kissed her hand, and left her.

'Sleep well,' he said kindly, as he might have spoken to a sick child.

But to Yseulte it seemed that she would never sleep again.

CHAPTER XLVIII.

For some days his world spoke only of the death of Platon Napraxine in the full vigour of his manhood. Men regretted him honestly, and many women mourned for him as sincerely, if with less disinterestedness. His body was taken to Zaraizoff, and there consigned to rest amidst the dust of his ancestors with all the pomp and splendour of a funeral, barbaric and gorgeous, like every other ceremony of his country. His mother and his little sons were there; his wife was absent. She had withdrawn herself to a secluded château in the Lake of Geneva, which had been the property of her father, and no one had access to her.

What did she feel? No one could know; scarcely could she have told, herself, so entangled and so conflicting were the emotions by which she was swayed. Two sentiments alone were distinct to her amidst the uncertainty of her thoughts; the one was regret that her last words had been to him words impatient and unkind; the other an intense rage against herself that by one involuntary question she had betrayed herself to Prince Ezarhédine. It had been the solitary moment in all her life in which anxiety had conquered her composure, and her perfect self-control had failed her.

After the day which brought the dead body of Napraxine to his house, and bore him up that beautiful staircase, where his heavy tread and his unlovely presence had so often seemed so unwelcome and so out of place, she had seen no one save those great ecclesiastics and high functionaries who were perforce admitted to her presence. Cards, dispatches, and letters were piled a foot deep in her ante-chamber, but she took no heed of any; her secretary had one formal reply with which he was instructed to receive one and all. Of the thousands who knew her throughout Europe, Othmar alone sent no word and made no sign.

She understood his silence.

She made no affectation of a woe she could not feel or be expected to feel; all the world had known how profound had been her indifference for her husband, and how often intolerant had been her dislike of him. But all that good taste and good breeding could dictate in respect to his memory she did; and she withdrew herself absolutely from the sights and sounds of the world in accordance with the severe usages of his country and with the tragic fate to which he had succumbed. For once her serenity had received a shock which, momentarily at least, affected and dispelled it; for once her languid observation of the ways of life and of death had been quickened to a dual feeling of mingled rejoicing and remorse. The sense of her own liberty was lovely to her, slight as had been the pressure of the bonds she wore; but her recognition of Platon Napraxine's character had never been so just or so warm as now when his living presence, his physical personality were no longer there to offend her taste and fret her patience. All the dispositions of his testament, all the entire trust they showed in her, all the immense possessions he bequeathed to her, touched her with that consciousness of magnanimity and generosity in this despised nature which had at times visited her during his lifetime, but had always been repulsed. Had it been possible for him to have returned to earth, he would have been as intolerable to her as before; but dead,—knowing that never more would he importune or trouble her with his unwelcome tenderness,—she remembered him with contrition and almost with remorse. The consciousness that never had she given him even one kind word in return for all his royal gifts and loyal worship hurt her sense of honour; when she remembered that the only praise she had ever accorded to him had only been part of a scene of dissimulation with which she had lulled his just suspicions, all the courage and candour which were natural to her rose up in her conscience and accused her of ingratitude and of treachery. Nor did she shrink from the *meâ culpâ* which her self-reproach exacted. She had never been a coward before her own conscience if her egoism had often made her sleep serenely, deaf to its voice. She did not disguise to herself that she had been neither merciful nor just to the dead man, neither worthy of his unquestioning confidence nor of his unmeasured devotion. She remembered many a time when a kind word would have cost her nothing and would have been so much to him. But, then, if she had spoken it, he would not have understood; he would have presumed on it; he would have imagined that it gave him every privilege; he had always been so stupid; he had never been able to understand *à demi-mot*—there had been no choice but to use the whip and chain to this poor blundering, fawning, loving hound, who would not otherwise comprehend how intolerable were his offered caresses.

Now the 'big dog' was dead and could never more offend.

Perhaps she had been harsh, she thought—sometimes.

In the solitude of the slow-coming chilly spring of the Canton de Vaud, Nadine Napraxine was left alone with her own thoughts. She remained in the strictest seclusion, willing to concede so much to the usages of her nation and the tragedy of his death. The isolation seemed very strange to her, accustomed as she was to have the most brilliant of societies, the most solicitous of courtiers, the most witty of associates, for ever about her. Her life had been always *dans le mouvement*, always seeking, if not always finding, distraction, always filled with the voices and the laughter of the world. In this complete solitude, where only her household were near her and there was no other sound than the fall of water, the burr of bees, the rush of a distant avalanche falling down the mountain side, or the lilt of a boatman's song echoing from the lake, it seemed to her as if it were she—or all the world—who was dead.

It had been suggested to her that she should have her children there, but she had rejected the idea instantly.

'Now that I am free,' she thought, 'for heaven's sake, let me forget the hours of my captivity if I can.'

They were well cared for; they should always be well cared for; she would never allow their interests to be neglected or their fortunes to be imperilled; but the sons of Platon Napraxine could never be more to her than the issue of a union she had loathed, the living records of a time of intense humiliation and disgust. Her retirement was not nominal; no guests passed her gates except those members of her husband's family and of her own whom it was impossible to refuse to see. Even they could not tell whether she rejoiced or grieved. She was serene and impassible; she never said a syllable which could let any light in upon her own emotions; when she spoke, if it were not with her usual malice, it was with all her usual skill at phrases which revealed her intelligence and hid her heart. She omitted none of the observances which Russian etiquette required from one in her position, and at the long religious services in honour of the dead she was careful to render the respect of her presence, though they meant no more to her than the buzzing of the bees in the laburnum and acacia flowers.

The tedious days passed monotonous and alike.

For the first time in her life she submitted to ennui without revolt; and if in the dewy silent evenings of the early summer she went down to the steps which overlooked the lake, and leaned there, and drew in the breath of the mountain air with a new invigorating sense of freedom from a burden which had for ever galled her, though she had borne it so lightly, no one was offended by that exhilaration, for no one was witness of it; even as no one, either, ever knew how in such evening musings as these an angry cloud would come upon her face and an impatient regret stir at her heart as she thought—why had not Othmar had patience?

She remembered him with a restless and unwilling tenderness.

The knowledge of how his name had escaped her to Ezarhédine was constantly present to her mind, and the recollection fretted and irritated her with all the mortification of a strong pride indignant at its own self-betrayal. Ezarhédine would, no doubt, relate the story of her momentary weakness to her friends and his. She had no belief in the discretion of men; they had their views and principles of honour, no doubt, but she had never known these remain superior to the impulses of their indiscretion or their inquisitiveness; they were always talkative as gossips round a market fountain, curious as children before a case of unpacked toys.

CHAPTER XLIX.

Whilst she was thus withdrawn from the world in the observance if not in the regrets of mourning, Othmar left Paris for the seclusion of the château of Amyôt.

The summer and the autumn months seemed to both him and Yseulte long and cruel; all the beauty of Amyôt in the blossoming hours could not make their life there happy to either of them. Since the death of Napraxine a great constraint had come between them. Each of them was sensible of thoughts and of emotions which neither would, or could, confide in the other.

Friederich Othmar came and went between Paris and the great Renaissance château, but he was powerless to alter what he deplored. There was not even any definite thing of which he could speak. There was no fault ever to be found in the gentleness and courtesy of Othmar to his wife; and there was no alteration in the deference and the docility which she always showed to him. Only there was something wanting: there was no spontaneity; there was no sympathy; there was none of that unspoken gladness which exhales from all real happiness as its fragrance from the rose. The wise old man said to himself, impatient and regretful, 'Why did Napraxine die? But for that, time would have been her friend. He would have grown used to her sweet presence, and habit would have brought content. But now!——'

Now, he knew that with every day which dawned, with every night which fell, Othmar brooded, night and day, over his lost future, destroyed by his own rash haste.

All his mind was with Nadine Napraxine, and it fretted him at times almost beyond endurance that he could see her and hear of her no more, know no more of her than all her world knew, or than the chronicles of the hour stated for public information. It seemed to him as it did to her, as if the strangest silence had fallen on the earth. He loved her infinitely more than he had ever done, intense and unscrupulous as had been the passion which she had aroused in him. She was entirely free; and he—he who had adored her—dared not even enter her antechamber or go where he could see her shadow fall upon the ground she trod!

The silence and the self-effacement of Yseulte were the most dangerous anodynes which he could have had. He dreamed his life away in visions of joys which never could be his, and the resignation of his young companion allowed him to dream on unroused.

Friederich Othmar saw his increasing preoccupation, his growing love of solitude, his impatience when he was recalled by force to the things of actual life, and he could have gnashed his teeth with rage and sorrow.

'He will never live out his years away from his sorceress,' he thought; 'and when they meet again, she will do what she chooses with him. If she like to make him the ridicule of Europe, he will accept his fate and deem it heaven. Whilst Yseulte—Yseulte,—before she is twenty, will be widowed in fact and left to the consolation of some little child, plucking the daisies on the sward here at her feet.'

To Friederich Othmar love had ever seemed the most puerile of delusions, the most illogical of all human fallacies, but now it took a deadlier shape before him, and he began to comprehend why poets—interpreters of human madness as they were—had likened it to the witch's mandrake, to the devouring sea, to the flame which no power can quench, to all things terrible, irresistible, and deadly as death.

Occasionally an impulse came to Yseulte to tell everything to Melville, who was not her confessor, but who had known all her people so well in their days of trial and adversity; but her pride repressed the instinct of confidence. Besides, she thought drearily, she knew well all that Melville would answer—the only reply, indeed, which would be possible to him in such a case—he would exhort her to patience, to hope, to trust in heaven and in her husband. The originality of his character would not be able to escape from the platitudes of custom; he would only say to her what she could say to herself, 'Be courageous and be calm; time often heals all woes.'

Sometimes, too, she thought wistfully that if she bore a living child perhaps she would reach some higher place in her husband's heart.

She had heard it often said that children formed a tie between those who were even indifferent to each other. At least—at least, she reflected, and strove to solace herself with this hope,—as the mother of a living child of his, she would be something in his house more than a mere form to wear his jewels and receive his indifferent caresses. Perhaps, she thought, if her eyes looked up at him from his child's face, he might grow to care for her a little. At least she would be something to him that Nadine Napraxine was not. It was a desolate kind of consolation to be the only one within reach of a girl scarce eighteen years old; a sadly forlorn and wistful hope; but it was something to sustain her in the midst of her perfect isolation of thought and suffering, and it prevented her abandonment to despair. She had one of those natures to which tenderness is more natural than passion; her character was of that gentle and serious kind which enables a woman to endure the desertion of her lover if the arms of a child are about her. And so she awaited the future patiently, without much trust in its mercies, yet not without courage and not wholly without hope.

'She looks very ill,' said the most observant of all her friends, Friederich Othmar, more than once to her husband. But Othmar replied that it was only the state of her health, and the elder man protested in vain.

'You think a girl of those years can be satisfied with bearing your children and being left alone in beautiful houses as a cardinal bird is shut up in a gilded cage?' he said irritably.

'She is certainly not left alone,' replied Othmar with annoyance; 'and I believe that she is precisely of that docile and religious temperament which will find the greatest enjoyment of existence in maternity. There are women formed for that kind of self-sacrifice beyond all others. She is one of them.'

'It is not the only sacrifice to which she is condemned!' muttered Friederich Othmar, but he feared to do more harm than good if he explained himself more clearly.

'Has she been complaining to you?' asked her husband with increasing anger.

'She would never complain,' returned his uncle positively. 'Besides, my dear Otho, whatever we may all think of you, to her you are a demi-god, the incarnation of all mortal and immortal excellences. She would as soon strike the silver Christ that hangs over her bed as consent to see a flaw in your perfections!'

Othmar only replied by an impatient gesture.

Both irritation and self-reproach were aroused in him, but they did no more than disquiet and annoy him. He saw no means by which he could be kinder, or gentler, or more generous, to Yseulte than he was already. Love was not his to command. He could not help it if day by day an unsatisfied passion gnawed in him for an absent woman, and if day by day the fair face of his young wife receded farther and farther from him into the shadowy distance of a complete indifference. All which he could compel himself to render,—consideration, deference, kindness, attention,—all these he poured out upon Yseulte with the utmost liberality. What was missing was not in his power to give. He felt with a shudder that the longer time went on, the more their lives passed together, the greater would grow the coldness he felt for her. He recognised all her sweetness and grace; he was not ungrateful for the affection she bore him; he admired the many delicate beauties of her mind and character. But she was nothing to him; she never would have the power to quicken his pulses by one second. She was all that purity, honour, and spirituality of thought could make her; but she had no place in his heart. He had even to struggle hard with himself at times not to let the sense of her perpetual presence there become almost an offence to him. He was a generous man, and he had always striven to be just, but he knew that he failed to be just to her because of the fret and fever of his own thoughts, which left him no peace, but kept repeating for ever the same burden: 'The woman you love is free now. O fool! O fool!'

He believed that he altogether concealed all that he felt from Yseulte. He did not dream that she had divined his secret. Her manner, which had never been demonstrative, but had been always marked by that mixture of shyness and of stateliness which were most natural to her, was not one which displayed the changes of every emotion; she had been reared in too perpetual a sense that it was both low and coarse to show the inner feelings of the heart by abrupt and transparent signs of emotion, and the calm high breeding of her habitual tone was as a mask, though a most innocent one, and hid alike her sorrow, her fear, her jealous terrors, and her wistful tenderness.

'I must never trouble him,' she said to herself again and again. She knew that she could not take away from him the burden of her life; that she could not release him from the vows he had vowed to her; but she did her uttermost to efface herself otherwise. In these tranquil summer months no one saw more amiss with her than a certain melancholy and lassitude, which were attributed to the state of her health. She was often alone, by choice, in the great gardens and the forest nooks of the park, and those poor little timid verses in which her soul found some kind of utterance were the only confidants of her grief and pain. They were poor things, she knew, but her heart spoke in them with involuntary, though feeble and halting, speech. They did her some little good. She had no mother or friend to whom she could say what she suffered, and from a priest she shrank; her woes—the mental woes of neglected love, the physical woes of approaching parturition—could not be told to any man.

'No one has wanted me all my life!' she thought one day, as she sat in the gardens of Amyôt, whilst her eyes filled with blinding tears. Her father had never heeded her; her grandmother had cared for her, indeed, but had willed her budding life to the cloister, as a thing for which there was no place amidst the love and the laughter of the earth. She had been dependent, undesired, on her cousin's charity, and to her husband she was as little as the does that couched at noon under his forest trees. No one had ever wanted her! The knowledge lay on her young life as a stone lies on the bird which it has killed. Through the hot mist of her tears she gazed wistfully at the long lines of the majestic house which only a year before had been to her the centre of such perfect happiness. And even that happiness he had never shared!

The hush of the golden noon-day was about her, and the perfume of innumerable roses filled the air.

'My little child will want me,' she thought, with a throb of hope at her heart.

After a little while she rose and walked towards the house. Othmar, who had come out from his library on to the terrace, saw her in the distance, and descended the steps to meet her.

'Do not tire yourself, my dear,' he said as he offered her his arm.

His very gentleness almost hurt her more than unkindness or discourtesy would have done. She seemed to see in it how he strove, by all the tenderness of outward ceremonial, to atone for the absence of all tenderness of the heart,—to pay so liberally in silver because he had no gold to give.

She had brushed her tears away before she had risen to return to the house; her features were calm, as usual, and if their expression was grave, that was not new with her. She had looked almost as much so on that first night when he had seen her sitting alone in the drawing-rooms of Millo.

As she walked beside him through the aisles of flowers in the sunshine of the brilliant noonday, she said, with her eyes lowered and her voice very low:

'If—if—I should die this time, would you remember always how much I have felt all your goodness to me? I cannot say all I feel—well—but I hope you would always believe how grateful I had been—when you should think of me at all.'

Othmar was touched and startled by the words.

'My dear child, do not speak so. Pray do not speak so,' he said, with real emotion. 'Send away such cruel thoughts. You must live long, and see your children's children running amidst these roses. You are hardly more than a child yourself in years even yet. And as for gratitude—that is not a word between us; what is mine is yours.'

'I want you to be sure of it—to never doubt it—if I die,' she said, in the same low, measured voice. 'I am always grateful.'

Then she withdrew her hand from his arm, and sat down for a moment on one of the marble seats beneath the great terrace. She looked over the wide sunlit landscape, the radiant gardens, the dark masses of the forests, the green plains and shining river far beyond. Her heart was full; words sprang to her lips, fraught with all the varying emotions of the past months. She longed to cry out to him, 'Ah, yes! You do not love me, I know!—I know! But is there nothing I could do? I would give my life, my soul——.'

But timidity and pride both held her mute. The moment passed; he never saw, as he might have seen, into her innocent heart if she had spoken.

The late autumn came, and her child was born as the first red leaves were blown upon the wind. But, enfeebled by the distress of her mind during so many months before its birth, it only breathed a little while the air of earth, then sank into death as a snowdrop sinks faded in the snow. The solace which she had looked to as a staff of comfort and of hope broke in two like a plucked reed.

An intense melancholy closed in upon her, from which no effort could rouse her. She said little; but when she rose from her bed and resumed her daily life, all alone in her heart was the one great grief which had now no hope to lighten it.

They strove to make her remember how young she was, what unspent years yet lay to her account, what undreamed-of treasures of new happiness were yet untouched by her; but nothing availed to give her any consolation.

The pale sunshine of the early winter found her white and chilled as itself. For she had a deeper pang than ever in her heart since she said ever to herself in her solitary grief: 'He does not care; he is good, he is gentle, he is compassionate; but he does not care.'

All her young life writhed in secret beneath that kindness which was only pitiful, that tenderness which was only conventional.

'I am nothing in his life,' she thought with tenfold bitterness. 'Nothing;— nothing;—nothing! Even for my child's death he does not really care!'

A woman far away, unseen, almost unheard of, was sole mistress of his existence. With all the terrible insight which a love forsaken and solitary possesses into the secrets of the life to which it clings, she read the thoughts and the emotions of Othmar as though they were written on some open page lit by a strong lamp. Although never a word of self-betrayal escaped him, never more than an involuntary gesture of lassitude or an unconscious sigh, she yet knew how utterly one recollection and one desire alone reigned over him and dominated him. She was no more a child, but was a woman humiliated, wounded, isolated, who suffered far the more because her wounds were not those which she could show, her humiliation was not such as she could reveal, and her isolation was one of the spirit, and not of the body.

'You must not mourn as those who have no hope,' said Melville to her, believing that her continued melancholy was due to the loss of her offspring. 'You are so young; you will have many other children; all kinds of joy will return to you, as their foliage will return to these leafless trees. Be grateful, my dear, to heaven for all the mercies which abide with you.'

She said nothing; but she turned her eyes on him one moment with an expression so heart-broken and weary that he was startled and alarmed.

'What grief can she have that we know not?' he marvelled. 'Othmar does not leave her; and he is the last man on earth to be cruel or even ungentle to a woman.'

For a moment he was tempted to refer his doubts to her husband; but, on reflection, he dared not. He had a sensitive fear of being deemed meddlesome, as priests so often are called; and it was difficult to make to Othmar—a very sensitive man, and at all times uncommunicative—so strange an accusation as would seem to lie in saying to him, 'The companion of your life is unhappy: what have you done?'

The winter in the country of the Orléannais grew very cold and damp; the rivers flooded many parts of the plains, and the end of the year menaced violent storms and widespread floods. Her physicians begged Yseulte to go elsewhere, and recommended a southern air; they spoke of S. Pharamond, and Othmar, though vaguely reluctant to go thither, consented, for he had no valid reason of refusal to give. To Yseulte herself any movement appeared indifferent; to whatever was proposed she always assented passively; the acquiescence of one whom no trifles or accidents of fate have power to hurt, and which belongs alike to perfect happiness and absolute despair.

Othmar would have given ten years of his life to have been able to go away by himself, to wander north, south, east, or west in solitary desolation, to be alone with his undying desires, and away from the innocent presence of a creature whom he knew that he wronged by every thought with which he rose at daybreak and lay down at night.

Yseulte had never been more to him than a sweet and tender-hearted child, whose personal beauties had for a little while beguiled him into the semblance of a faint passion, into a momentary semi-oblivion, always imperfect and evanescent. But now, quiet as she was, and careful as she was never to betray herself, nevertheless a constant reproach seemed to look at him from her eyes, and her continual vicinity seemed as continual a rebuke. He was not a man, as many are, who could lightly neglect or deceive a woman; he was incapable of the half-unconscious cruelty with which many men, when their fancy has passed, leave the object of it in pitiable solitude, to console herself as best she can; he had too much sensitiveness and too much sense of chivalrous obligation to deny, even to his own reflections, the claims which his wife had on him for sympathy and affection. That he could not give them to her, because all his heart and soul and mind were with another woman, burdened him with a perpetual sense of injustice and offence done to her. He had sought her; he had taken her life voluntarily into his; he knew that it would be a treachery and a baseness to fail in his duty towards her. For that very reason her daily presence galled him almost beyond endurance, and, though he forced himself to remain beside her and to preserve to her every outward semblance of regard, his whole life chafed and rebelled, as the horse frets which is tied in stall to its manger, whilst all its longing is for the liberty of the pasture and the air.

If Melville had followed his impulse and said to him, 'What fault can there be in her?' he would have answered truthfully, 'None: all the fault is my own;' and he would have thought in secret: 'She has that involuntary fault which is the cruellest of all others: she is not the woman I love!'

He had to put strong constraint upon himself not to shrink from the sound of her gentle voice, not to avoid the glance of her wistful eyes; he was afraid that she should read the truth of his own utter indifference in his regard; he felt with horror of himself that it was even growing something greater, something worse, than mere indifference; that soon, do what he would, he would be only able to see in her the barrier betwixt himself and the fate he coveted.

'Good God! what miserable creatures we are!' he thought. 'I meant, as honestly as a man could ever mean anything, to make that poor child's days as perfect in happiness as mortal life can be, and all I have actually done is to sacrifice uselessly both her and myself! Heaven send that she may never find it out herself!'

He was far from suspecting that she had already discovered the truth. All the fine prescience, the quickness at reading trivial signs and forming from them far-reaching conclusions, which love lends to the dullest were absent from him, because love itself was absent. Her pride gave her a sure mask, and he had not the lover's impulse which looks for the face beneath.

Their lives outwardly passed in apparent unison and sympathy. He seldom left her save when any urgent matter took him for a brief space to Paris or some other European capital, and the days passed as evenly and unmarked by any event at the château of S. Pharamond as at that of Amyôt. People of a conspicuous position can seldom enjoy solitude, and the demands of society provide them with a refuge from themselves if embarrassment has forced them to need one. Othmar, who had at no time been willing to open the doors of his house to the world, now became almost solicitous to have the world about him. It spared him that *solitude à deux* which, so exquisite to the lover and to the beloved, is so intolerable to the man who knows that he is loved but has no feeling to bestow in answer. Throughout the early winter months they were seldom or never alone. Yseulte said nothing when he urged her to surround herself with people, but obeyed with a sinking heart. She was very proud; she remained tranquil and gentle in manner to him and to everyone, and, if she were at times more pensive than suited her years or her world, it was attributed by all who knew her to the loss of her child. She grew thin and white, and was always very grave; but she had so admirable a courtesy, so patient a smile for all, that not a soul ever dreamed her heart was breaking in her breast.

Sometimes when she was quite alone she wandered up the hill-side beneath the olive trees to the bastide of Nicole Sandroz, and sat amidst the blossoming violets, the tufts of hepaticas, with a strange dull wonder in her at herself. Could it be only two years ago since she had seen Othmar coming in the dusk beneath the silvery boughs and had learned on the morrow that he had asked her hand in marriage?

Nicole watched her wistfully, but she, too, who had lost her *petiot* in the days of her youth, believed that the melancholy which she saw in her darling was due to the death of her offspring. She strove, in ruder words, but in the same sense, to console her as Melville had done. Yseulte smiled gently, thanked her, and said nothing. What was the use, she mused, of their speaking to her of the future? The future, whatever else it brought, would only take the heart and the thoughts of her husband farther and farther from her. She knew still but little of the world, but she knew enough to be conscious that the woman who fails in the early hours of her marriage to make her husband her lover will never in the years to come find him aught except a stranger. All the sensitive hauteur of her nature shrank from the caresses which she knew were only inspired by a sense of pity or of duty. She drew herself more and more coldly away from him, whilst yet the mere sound of his voice in the distance made all her being thrill and tremble. And he was too grateful for the relief to seek to resist her alienation.

He did not guess, because he did not care to guess, that she loved him so intensely that she would stand hidden for hours merely to see him pass through the gardens or ascend the sea stairs of the little quay. Her timidity had always veiled from him the intensity of her affections, and now her pride had drawn a double screen between them.

'He only pitied me then!' she thought, as she sat amongst the violets at Nicole's flower farm. 'He only pities me now!'

Pity seemed to this daughter of a great race the last of insult, the *obole* thrown to the beggar which brands him as beggar for evermore.

'I was hungered, and he gave me bread; I was homeless, and he sheltered me!' she said, in the agony of her heart. 'And I—I thought that love!'

CHAPTER L.

With the turn of the year and the springing of the crocuses her cousins had come to Millo. When she was in their presence she was more careful than at any other time that no one should see in her any pain which could be construed by them into a reproach against Othmar.

'She grows proud and cold,' said the Duchesse. 'The women of her blood have always been like that—religious and austere. It is a pity. It will age her before her time; and it is not at all liked in the world nowadays—save just at Lent.'

Blanchette, with her keen mysotis-coloured eyes, saw farther than her mother saw. She did not dare to tease her cousin, or to banter her, but she looked sometimes with curiosity and wonder in her face.

One day, in a softer mood than was usual with her, she came over the gardens from Millo and found her way to her cousin. Blanchette liked to be welcome at S. Pharamond; her shrewd little senses smelt the fragrance in all wealth which dogs find in the truffle; she was always asking for things and getting them, and though she was afraid of Othmar as far as she could be of anyone, she retained amongst her respect for Yseulte's position her derision for what she termed her romanticism, her Puritanism, and her habitual ignorance of how to extract the honey of self-indulgence from the flowers of pleasure. But Blanchette had all the wisdom of the world in her little fair, curly head, and though at times her malicious impulses conquered her judgment, she usually repressed them out of reverence for the many good gifts which fell to her from her cousin's hands, and those instincts of 'modernity' which forced her to worship where so much riches were.

She came into the garden salon this day, the one where Melville had once said to Othmar that to make a home was in the power of any man not a priest. Her eyes were watchful and her manner important; but Yseulte, to whom the child's presence was always irksome, though her gratitude to their mother forced her always to receive the little sisters with apparent willingness, had not observation enough, or thought enough of her, to notice those signs. She was alone; it was two hours after the noon breakfast; Othmar was away, she knew not where; he had gone out early in the forenoon. She was lost in the weariness of those thoughts which occupied her unceasingly, when the pretty gay figure of the child tripped up to her side, and the thin high voice of her began its endless chatter.

'They were talking about you yesterday after the *déjeuner*,' she said, after her discursive gossip had embraced every subject and person then of interest to her, pecking at each one of them furtively, petulantly, as a well-fed mouse pecks at crumbs of cake. 'They were saying how beautiful you were; even mamma said that, and they all agreed that if only you were not so grave, so cold, so almost stiff, nobody would be admired more than you. But men think you do not care, so they do not care. It is true,' added Blanchette, studying the face of her cousin out of the corner of her eye, 'it is true that the Princess Napraxine, whom they are always so mad about, is just as indifferent too. But then it is another kind of indifference—hers. She is always provoking them with it, on purpose. You go through a room as if you were saying a paternoster under your breath. It is a great difference——'

'It is, no doubt, a great difference,' said Yseulte, with more bitterness than she was aware of; the idle words struck at the hidden wound within her. The difference was vast indeed between herself and the woman whom her husband loved!

Blanchette watched her sharply, herself sitting on a stool at her feet.

'Do you know,' she said, pulling the ears of Yseulte's great dog, 'that she is coming—indeed, I think, is here? I heard them say so yesterday. It seems that the Prince bought that little villa and gave it to her—La Jacquemerille—when they were here two years ago. She is very rich, you know. Her husband has left her such immense properties, and then I think she had a great deal of money all of her own, before his death, from some distant relative, who left it to her because she did not want it; it is always like that.'

Yseulte rose abruptly. Blanchette could not see her face, but she saw her left hand, which trembled.

As far as the child liked anyone, she was attached to her cousin; since her marriage Yseulte had been extremely generous and kind to her, and the selfish little heart of Blanchette had been won, as far as ever it could be won, by its affections which were only another form of selfishness. She had been unable to resist the temptation of telling her news, and saying what was unkind; and yet in her way she was compassionate.

'Why are you so very still and grave?' she said now after a pause. 'They say it is because the child died, but that cannot be it; it is nonsense; you would not care like that. Do you know now what I think? Do not be angry. I think that you are so unhappy because—because—now Prince Napraxine is dead, you fancy that she would have been his wife if you had not been here!'

'Silence!' said Yseulte, with imperative command. Her face grew scarlet under the inquisitive, searching gaze of the child. She suffered an intolerable humiliation beneath that impertinent and unerring examination which darted straight into her carefully-treasured secret, and dragged it out into the light of day.

'Ah!' said Blanchette, with what was, for her, almost regret and almost sympathy, 'ah, I was sure of it! I have always been sorry that I said anything to you that day. But why do you care? If I were you, I should not care. What does it matter what he wishes? Men always wish for what they cannot get; I have heard that said a hundred and a thousand times. And you are his wife, and you have all the houses, and all the jewels, and all the horses; and all the millions; and as he is always thinking of her, so people say, he will not mind what you do. You may amuse yourself just as you like. If I were you, I should go and play at the tables.'

'Silence! You are insolent; you hurt me; you offend me,' said Yseulte, with greater passion than she had ever yielded to in all her life. All the coarse consolations which the world would have given her, repeated and exaggerated on the worldly-wise lips of Blanchette, seemed to her the most horrible parody of her own sacred and intolerable woe, so carefully buried, as she thought, from any human eye.

'It is true,' said the child, offended and sullen. 'Everyone knew he never loved you; he always loved her. Even in Paris last year——. But what does it matter? You have got everything you can want——'

But Yseulte had left her standing alone in the golden-coloured drawing-room of S. Pharamond, with the irises and roses so gaily broidered on the panels of plush.

Blanchette shrugged her shoulders as she glanced round the room. 'What idiots are these sensitives!' she thought, with wondering contempt. 'What can it matter? She has all the millions——'

The mind of the little daughter of the latter half of the nineteenth century could go no farther than that.

She had all the millions!

She had meant, quite sincerely, to give sympathy and consolation, but she could not help fashioning both in her own likeness.

Yseulte, with a feverish instinct to reach solitude and the open air, left her tormentor within the house, and hastily covering herself, passed out into the gardens of S. Pharamond, and walked farther and faster than her physical strength, which had not been great since the birth of her child, was well fitted to bear. She longed thirstily for the grey skies and the moist air of Faïel, for the cold dusky seas of the north-west and the dim far-stretching lands. The light, the buoyancy, the glitter, the dry clear atmosphere of those southern shores, oppressed her and fevered her. If she had not altogether lost the habit of confidence in her husband, she would have said to him, 'I sicken of all this drought and cloying sweetness. Let me go where the west wind blows; where the northern billows roll; where it is cold, and dusk, and green, and full of shadows; where it does not mock one's pain with light and laughter!'

But she had lost that habit utterly: she never spoke of anything she felt or wished; she accepted all the days of her life as they came to her.

'I have nothing of my own,' she thought; 'I have no right to wish for anything.'

He had made this place hers; he always spoke of it as hers; it was, indeed, her own inalienably; but she did not feel it to be so. It was only a part of his wide charity to her—the charity which she had thought was love.

She walked far, she scarcely knew herself where, taking her way mechanically through the grounds and into the fields and orange woods adjoining them, following the windings of the paths which wound upward between the great gnarled trunks of olives and beneath their hoary branches. As she ascended under the forest of olives, which was part of the lands of S. Pharamond, she could see below her a broad hunting road, cut in old times by the Maison de Savoie, neglected by the Commune, but kept in preservation by Othmar himself. She heard a sound of horses' hoofs, and instinctively looked down; between the network of olive boughs she saw a low carriage, drawn by three black ponies abreast, and harnessed in the Russian manner, their abundant manes streaming on the wind as they dashed headlong down the steep incline. They were followed by two outriders in liveries of deep mourning.

The woman who drove them looked upward, and made a slight salutation with a smile.

It was Nadine Napraxine.

In another instant the turn of the road hid them from sight, and the beat of the galloping hoofs was lost in the sound of a little torrent which fell down through the red bare rocks above, and fed with its moisture the beds of violets beneath the olives.

CHAPTER LI.

That night there was a concert at Millo. It was the fifth week of Lent: nothing was possible but a musical party. There were famous musicians and equally famous singers; the gardens were illumined, and the whole arrangements had that charm and novelty which Madame de Vannes knew so well how to give to all she did. But the evening was chiefly noticeable for the first appearance in the world, since her husband's death, of the Princess Napraxine. She came late, as she always came everywhere; she still wore black; there was no relief to it anywhere, except that given by the dazzling whiteness of her great pearls and of her beautiful skin. The contour of her throat and bosom, the exceeding beauty of her arms, had never been seen in such marked perfection as in that contrast with the sombre robe she wore, sleeveless, and fastened on each shoulder only with a clasp of pearls. One unanimous chorus of admiration ran from mouth to mouth as she entered.

The tragedy of her husband's death had left no trace on her. Her smile had its old ironical insouciance, her lips their rich warm rose-colour, her eyes their lustrous languor; abstinence from all the fatigues of society, and the fresh air of the country life in which she had passed the tedious months of her seclusion, had given her all the vivifying forces of health without destroying that look of fragility and languor which were her most potent charms.

'Poor Napraxine!' thought Melville as he looked at her; but he was the only one there who remembered the dead man.

Neither Othmar nor his wife was present there that night.

Both feared, with a fear which lay mute at the heart of each, to see again for the first time before the eyes of the world the woman whose memory ruled his life.

CHAPTER LII.

When Nadine Napraxine returned home that night she found a letter lying on the table, of whose superscription she recognised the writing.

'So soon!' she thought, with her little smile, which had always been so calm and so amused before the madnesses of men.

But when she had read it, it seemed like a living, burning, palpitating thing, so did its words throb and thrill with ardour, reproach, and pain. All the suffering and passion pent up in his soul for twelve long months had broken loose and were uttered in it.

He had written in the silence of the dawn, when all the world was quiet as the grave, and the loud beating of his heart was audible to his own ear as he realised that near him, beyond those few miles of feathery foliage and flower-scented fields, there lay sleeping the one woman he adored. The impulse to write so to her had been stronger than himself, and all wisdom, manhood, and pride spoke to him in vain. To her alone had he ever laid bare his heart; to her alone was he not ashamed to uncover all its weakness, all its rebellion, all its futile and feverish pain. Let her laugh if she would, he thought, but let her know all he suffered through her. For a year he had kept silent; chained down by the bonds of duty and of custom. For a year he had lived out his dreary days as best he might, bearing his burden mutely, and striving to do his best; but at the knowledge that she was near him, there in the pale, cool air of the daybreak, all his efforts at self-command were shattered as silk threads break in a nervous hand.

No one had ever written to her as he wrote now.

She read the letter, with the rosy light of the morning coming in through her half-closed shutters; and the words of it banished the sleep which hung like vapour about her languid eyes and her dreamy thoughts. The smile went away from her lips. The force of another human heart smote for once an echo from hers.

'What madness!' she murmured.

But it was a madness which seemed noble to her, beautiful in its folly, and even in its torture; she felt a strange emotion as she read and re-read the only message which he had sent to her in the whole months of a year. She sat lost in thought; hesitation was rare with her, but now she hesitated. With a word she could banish him for ever from her life. With a word she could call him for ever to her side. His face seemed to rise before her as she looked at the signature of his name; his voice seemed in her ear pleading, imperious, tender, as she had heard it a hundred times. A year had been lost; a year had passed and dropped in the past, and they had never looked upon each other's faces. A certain emotion which she had never known stirred in her,—the weakness of a sudden yearning, of a sudden wistful desire.

'Is this love too?' she thought, with that ironical doubt of herself with which she had so often doubted others.

'I have never cared,' she thought, with scorn for the impulses which had moved her. But she cared now. The silence and the absence of those long months had been his friends. In her meditations she had confessed to herself that he had not been to her the mere poor slave and spaniel that other men had been; she had thought to herself more than once with a wonder at her own regret: 'If he had only had patience! If he had only waited!'

She read the letter he had written twice again. Then she burned it. She did not need to keep it. Each word of it was written on her memory. When the day was warm with the light of the forenoon's sunshine she went out into the air. She felt the need of movement, of space, of a fresh atmosphere. For the first time in her life a certain excitation had taken the place of her tranquil serenity. A certain restlessness had disturbed her indifference; she had the sense of having descended to some too great concession, of having let herself fall from her serene heights of power to some human feebleness and frailty.

'If this be love?' she mused again with doubt and disdain, casting on the awakening warmth of her own feelings that ice of scepticism with which she had so often frozen the hearts of others. 'If I were only quite sure of what I feel,' she thought, with that egoism which was so natural to her that it was part of her every impulse and of her every motive.

Life had a certain loveliness for her in her perfect liberty, though she still doubted whether its monotony would not mar even that. The sense of her entire freedom was still welcome to her, and the world awaited her as a courtier, hat in hand, awaits his queen. All its pleasures,—such as they were, she knew them all, and held them in slight esteem,—would be hers. She had youth, beauty, and wit, and, when the first two of these should have left her, would still have that power of great riches which, as a wise man has said, is the only one to which the modern world will bow. And yet a vague melancholy was upon her; that melancholy, like a light mist on a smiling landscape, which she had once said might have made her such a poet as Maikoff had she lived for ever in the solitude of the steppes.

She went out into the balmy air, clear as a crystal, and filled with the scent of blossoming orange-boughs. She stood awhile on the marble terrace and looked seaward. The memories of the dead men who so late had been living there beside her passed over her in the warmth and light of the morning with a chill, as the north wind will sweep through the sunshine and scatter the clusters of orange-buds. Of them all, it was of her husband that she thought with the nearest likeness to self-reproach which her nature made possible.

'He was brave, he was as trustful as a dog, he was *bon enfant*,' she mused, 'and I do not think I ever said to him a single kind word before that last day—and then it was only said to deceive him!'

She remembered him as he had spoken to her on that day. He had had a certain dignity, the dignity of manliness, of simplicity, of truthfulness; and all that was left of him was lying, mere dry dust and bones, in his emblazoned coffin in the gilded gloom of the church at Zaraizoff.

'Well—the dead are dead, and we shall soon be with them,' she thought with a sigh, as she turned from the sea wall of the terrace and looked at the picturesque and irregular front of the house, covered with its gay garlands of creeping plants.

The place was hers, bought for her by Napraxine, as one may buy a bonbon-box for a child. It seemed that day to laugh with light and colour. Coming hither as she did from the endless night of a Russian winter, it seemed bathed in heat, and luminance, and flowers. She descended the steps to where her ponies waited, and went with them along the climbing roads into the hills above La Jacquemerille.

The day was still young. The bare mountain sides wore the hues of the jacinth and amethyst; the odours of sweet herbs and spring flowers were strong and sweet; far down below, unseen, the sea was sparkling, lending the sense of its presence and its freedom to all the gorges and hillsides above. Her swift-footed ponies bore her fleetly as the Hours bore Aurora through the roseate and golden radiance of the April morning.

With intention she guided them up the steep roads which led to the humble church of S. Pharamond, hidden beneath its great gnarled olive trees, and covered with its network of rose-boughs. She knew that Yseulte went there often in the forenoon, and the caprice moved her to see if she could meet, as if by chance, this poor child, whose fate lay in the hollow of her hand, like a bird taken from a trap to be strangled with a touch at pleasure of its keeper. The sense of such power was always sweet to her; although so familiar, its familiarity did not detract from its pleasure. It was the sole thing which did not by repetition grow monotonous. Her life had been short by years, but it had been full of such dominion. She had dealt with men and women as she chose, and to make or mar their destinies had always been the sole pastime of which she did not weary. Humanity was her box of puppets, as it is that of the Solitary of Varzin. To hold the strings of fate, to bind and loose the threads of circumstance, and weave the warp and woof of destiny, was the only science which had ever had charm over her changeful temperament and her sceptical intelligence. Beside it all other things were trivial and tame. She had never met anyone who had resisted her will; Othmar himself had done so for awhile, but he had lived to repent and to succumb.

The church of S. Pharamond was empty and silent; there was no office said that day; it was grey and still and mournful, and no living thing was in it save a swallow perched upon the altar rail. She pursued the steep hillside road, overhung with olive and fig trees, the wayside carpeted with gladiolus and the blue fleur-de-luce. Below, through the light green foam of spring foliage and the sombre masses of pine and ilex woods, there rose the towers and pinnacles of the château, rising slim and fantastic, against the azure of the sky. Around her the silence was unbroken, except by a tethered goat cropping euphorbia and ivy from a ruined wall.

Looking through the boughs of the olives, she saw afar off the figure of Yseulte. Where she was standing was on the land of Nicole Sandroz, the furrows, thick with flowers, climbing the hill slope, the orchard of lemon and olive hiding the low white walls of the house. She alighted, and left her little horses standing by a stone well made in the old wall where the goat was tethered. She wished to see the wife of Othmar, and she moved straight towards her where she sat beneath one of the gigantic olives, whose foliage spread in a misty cloud silvery and sea-green above her. She had uncovered her head in the deep shadow around her; her attitude was listless, spiritless, dejected; in the shade thrown from the olive boughs her face looked very colourless, worn, and thin. All her look of childhood had passed away, and almost all her youth as well. As she recognised her rival she trembled violently and rose to her feet, losing for the moment all self-control and presence of mind. Her large brown eyes dilated with fear, like a deer's when it is hard pressed in the chase. She had scarcely self-command to make the common gesture of salutation.

Nadine Napraxine, smiling, approached her and looked at her with that critical and penetrating glance which, through its languor, could read all the secrets of the soul. She spoke the bland commonplaces of compliment and courtesy with her sweetest manner, her most gracious grace; and the girl, paralysed once again, as a hundred times before, murmured a stupid sentence or so, coloured, grew pale, hesitated, felt herself awkward, foolish, and constrained, and could not keep down the tremor which shook her from head to foot, thus suddenly confronted with the woman whom her husband loved. All the terror which she had felt in Paris returned to her with tenfold more suffering, tenfold more intensity. In the morning light, standing amongst the simple wild herbs and flowers, her foe had the same magical power of magnetism over her as she had had in the lighted drawing-rooms and theatres of Paris. She understood why she herself was nothing in her husband's life, and this other was all.

With simple gracious words, as she might have spoken to a timid child, her enemy continued to address her, passing over her constraint and silence as though she perceived them not, and all the while that the smooth, careless phrases rose so easily on her lips she studied the changing colour and the frightened eyes of Yseulte with that amused and merciless analysis which was so common to her. She understood how all the whole being of her victim shrank from her as a bird shrinks from the gaze of a snake, yet how her courage and her pride strove with her emotion and vainly tried to hide her fear.

'Oh, foolish, foolish child!' she thought, from the height of her own assured strength, her own irresistible power. 'If you mistrust yourself, you lie at the mercy of all your foes. Do you not know that the first necessity for all success is to believe in our own power to attain it? Nature has given you personal loveliness, but the gift is of no more use to you than a score of music in the hands of an ignorant who cannot read it, than a sculptor's chisel in the fingers of a child. You love Othmar, and you weep for him; and you know how to do nothing more. Do you suppose that women govern men with tears? Do you suppose that their desires wake because a woman prays?'

There was derision, but there was a not unkind pity in her, as her eyes studied the face in which, despite its youth and delicacy and charm, Othmar could see no beauty.

'Your child died?' she said suddenly, as she sat there beside her unwilling and trembling captive. Yseulte bent her head; she could not trust her voice to answer.

'Did you care so much?' said Nadine Napraxine in wonder.

'I wished that it had been myself.'

The words escaped her almost unawares. When they had been uttered she longed to recall them. They would sound, she knew, like a confession of sorrow to the ear of one to whom all the sorrow of her life was due.

'Are you not happy, then, my dear?' said Nadine Napraxine: her tone was grave and soft, and had for once no mockery or innuendo in it.

Yseulte grew paler even than she had been before; a frown of anger knitted her fair brow; her expression grew cold and hard.

'I think you have no right to ask me that,' she said, gathering with effort courage enough to oppose her dreaded foe. 'I think you have no right. You are my husband's friend, not mine.'

Nadine Napraxine smiled.

'The frightened doe has its own bravery when roused,' she mused; and aloud she only said, with all the sweet suave courtesy of her very gentlest manner:

'His friend and yours. Surely that is the same thing? Or if it be not, you should be wise and make it so.'

She paused a moment, then added softly still:

'Happiness only comes to the wise, my dear; it does not come to those who stake their all upon one cast like the mad gamblers in the *salle de jeu* behind those hills. But you are too young to understand; and if I spoke to you all day I should not teach you my philosophies.'

'I do not wish to learn them.'

She spoke almost sullenly, almost rudely, as the natural courage of her temper asserted itself and strove to struggle against the paralysis of mesmerised fear in which the presence of her rival held her.

'They have been useful,' said Nadine Napraxine with a chillier intonation. 'And for want of them, what have women—who can only love—made of their lives, and of their lovers? But since you will not allow that I am your friend, I will leave you to your sylvan solitudes. Adieu, my dear. It is not in the woods and hills that you will learn to recover that *secret de bonheur* which you have lost so early.'

She lingered a moment, looking at Yseulte with her meditative, languid, unrevealing gaze. The girl's lips trembled, her throat swelled, her eyes filled with scorching tears; she turned abruptly away lest her self-control should altogether fail her. She knew that she had betrayed herself as utterly to her enemy's eyes as though she had poured out in words all the piteous secrets of her aching heart. Nadine Napraxine passed slowly beneath the olive branches, brushing the humble flowers with her careless sovereign's step.

'She is foolish, she is simple, she is awkward, and she is most unwise,' she thought. 'But she is brave——'

It was the quality which she always honoured.

CHAPTER LIII.

When she returned home, she shut herself in her own rooms, and was not seen, even by her women, for three hours. She lay almost immovable upon a couch, whilst the sunshine came tempered and rose-hued through the lowered awnings of her windows, and the air around her was filled with the scent of hundreds of cut roses placed in all the jars and bowls and vases in her sight. For the first time in her life a doubt which came from pity, and a hesitation which came from conscience, were at war with all her habits, instincts, and vanities. Underneath her egoism, and her cruelty, and her many ironies, there had always been latent a disdainful honour. Once having given it, she would have kept her word to the meanest creature; she would have taken no advantage of the weakest enemy, if to do so had been an injustice. She was capricious in every act of her life, but her caprices had no meanness in them; she was supremely merciless, because she was supremely indifferent, but she was capable of perfect loyalty in her own fashion. Far down in the depths of her complex nature there was, beneath all the coldness, malice and selfishness of disposition and of custom, a vague instinct of chivalrous generosity. If ever that chord in her were touched it always responded. When she had been a child, reading the old chronicles in her father's library, her favourite of history had always been John of France, for sake of that voluntary return to his captivity in England.

She comprehended the delirious impulse on which Othmar, hearing that she was near him after twelve months of absence, had been unable to control the emotion which mastered him, and had, in an hour of irresponsible passion, laid his soul bare before her, in all its weakness, and offered to load it with any weight she chose, so that only he could be once more admitted to her presence. And she knew, even more surely than he did, because she was calmer than he was, all which hung upon her own decision. She knew that, once entering there, he would be then and for ever hers; never more his wife's. She was too clear of sight to cheat herself with self-delusions. Othmar would be faithful to her, and false to all else all his life through, if once she wrote to him the simple word he asked for: 'Come.' She knew that he had played with fire unharmed, only because she herself had been cold as ice; but now her coldness seemed suddenly to melt within her, and her heart to go out to him in sweet and sudden yearning.

If he came there he would come as her lover.

To all her newly awakening tenderness, and to all her habitual instincts of supremacy, the temptation was strong. For once in her life she realised something of the force of that irresistible and enervating impulse which heretofore had always seemed to her a mere frenzy of ungoverned senses, of disordered dreams. For once her life seemed incomplete if lived on without his.

Her irony and raillery could not aid her against herself; she was absorbed in, and invaded by a tide of new and warm emotion; the words which he had written to her seemed burned into her mind—seemed to fill the rose-scented air, and become audible, as though his voice were pleading to her.

'If this be love?' she thought again, with astonished impatience, with a sense of servitude and weakness.

Twice she rose to write the one word he asked; and twice she put the pen aside with it unwritten.

Such vacillation was new to her, and hateful as a sign of feebleness. Her caprices had been as changeful as the winds of April, but beneath them her will had been always firm as a rod of steel, centred ever on her own whim and pleasure. Now she was irresolute, and scarce knew what she wished, or what she chose.

She who had the blood in her of lascivious empresses, and of fierce murderers of men, was swayed by two unfamiliar and divided things—by conscience, and compassion. The tide of freshly-roused emotions, which would have swept her onward to the gratification of them without thought or pause, was checked by a sentiment as rare—the sentiment of mercy. Once, one of her people, in the dark days of Natalia Narischkine's rule, being of those who slew in the name of the idiot, Ivan, had slaughtered the Narischkine right and left, not pausing for age or youth, or sex, but, coming to the place where a young child of the hated race lay sleeping, had dropped his blood-red sword in shame, as before some holy image, faltered, and turned away; the child had slept on unharmed. Such hesitation as that was with her now, born out of the very faults of her nature, out of her disdain, of her hauteur, of her superb self-love.

She was conscious of a desire to be in the presence of Othmar, to hear his voice, to see his face again; a desire enervating, vague, full of a dangerous languor, and a dangerous warmth; beyond that, stimulating and sustaining it, were the instincts of empire, of dominion, of a capricious and ever-victorious volition. Never in all her life had she resisted an impulse of self-indulgence, had she hesitated before any sacrifice of others. Absence had increased the shadowy attraction which had always drawn her towards this one amongst her many lovers; in the long silent months of her solitude his memory had grown dearer and more welcome with each day. And he was hers, if she chose.

At her command all honour, duty and allegiance would be mere empty words on his ear, without power to hold him, or meaning to move him. Dignity, self-respect, and loyalty to his self-chosen vows would become no more to him than threads of silk upon the neck of a courser broke loose. She had only to let him enter there, and the world would hold nothing for him but herself.

And for once she might perchance be able to share that oblivion, to comprehend that ecstasy; and yet she hesitated, because a new faint sense of pity and of compassion had come upon her.

'After all,' she thought, 'I should probably care such a little while, and she, poor child,—it is all her life!'

A disdainful compassion forbade her to strike down so weak a foe. Opposition or conflict would have intensified all her imperious resolve, and heightened the zest of her power of destruction; but the helplessness, the feebleness of her rival disarmed her. It would be like striking a nesting-bird, a wounded kid.

Nadine Napraxine thought of her with a sensation of pity and the stronger sensation of disdain which was inevitable to her character. A creature who could not conquer, could not resist, could not keep hold upon her own, seemed a thing so foolish and so feeble to her! Even in her solitude, her imperial supremacy made her lips smile contemptuously, her eyes gleam with scorn, as she rose and paced her chamber for a few moments, her head erect and her bosom risen high with her proud thoughts.

All the superb courage and scorn which were much stronger in her than any other emotion, rejected so easy a victory, so sure a triumph.

'She is so impotent, poor little fool!' she murmured. 'She will break her heart for ever in vain; she will never touch his.'

Her rooms were filled with the sweet faint smell of the roses, and heated to the heat of a midsummer noon. She sat still in the dreamy warmth, and all her vague regrets oppressed her with a faint, heavy sense of inclinations suppressed, and impulses awaking after long torpor.

'I should not hesitate at a crime,' she thought, 'but this would be almost a baseness.'

And her memory went once more back to the hour in which the dead body of Napraxine had been before her sight, the tea-rose held close in his stiffened hand, and darkly red with the blood of his lungs.

'If he were living'—she thought.

If he had been living, he could have avenged Yseulte and himself.

But he was dead, a thing of bones and ashes—powerless, senseless, defenceless. Something in that dishonour which would be done to a dead man and to a helpless child seemed to her courage cowardice, to her generosity meanness, to her dignity unworthiness.

'Neither could ever hurt us,' she thought, 'neither could ever avenge it on us.'

Her sense of the utter impotency of those two, when she remembered it, disarmed her where opposition or the struggle of forces equal to her own would have made her obstinate and pitiless. They were so helpless! the girl, in her pathetic, ignorant, unloved humiliation and ineptitude; the man, dead in his strength, who had left only a memory behind him. It would be as easy to sweep the one out of her path as to forget and deride the other; so easy that it seemed not worth the while; so easy that it seemed almost base.

She would have used her blade of steel without mercy to cleave through bone and flesh of any who should have ventured to oppose her; but to cut down a garden lily already dying of drought, to strike a pale shadow from the tomb—it seemed poor, unworthy.

Othmar was hers if she would.

Had there been any doubt of it, her nature would have urged her on in unsparing resolution until he should have yielded. But he was hers when she chose, body and soul, peace and honour, present and future. Her perfect sense of empire and security of dominion left her serene and gentle; she could listen to the voice of pity, the impulse of what men, in their stupidity, called conscience. It was with the disdainful generosity with which the Great Katherine might have loosed one of her lovers from the chains which bound him to her throne, that she renounced her power to take him from his wife.

'If it were only a crime,' she thought, in the mystical complex subtleties and intricacies of her brain, 'if it were only a crime, the darkness would heighten the dawn, the danger would sweeten the pleasure, the courage of it would strengthen the self-indulgence; but when it is mean, when one is sure that there is no one living who can avenge it, only a poor meek fool who will weep——!'

The laws of so-called duty said nothing to her.

The morality of the world was in her sight a mere mass of affectation, hypocrisies, and timorous shifts.

To her sated and ever-curious intelligence a crime might have had some potent charm, because it would have possessed some novelty and proffered some strange experience.

But a meanness revolted her with the same sense of disgust as would have moved her before squalor or disease. The same impulse which moves the white-plumaged bird to keep aloof from dust or mud, moved her to recoil from what was base or was ungenerous.

She rose and approached one of the windows, and pushed the rose-coloured blind aside, and looked out over the wide white marble terrace and the blue silent sea beyond.

It was three in the afternoon.

He had waited ten hours for her answer.

She left the casement and sat down and wrote. She wrote rapidly, as her wont was; and when she had written, folded and sealed her letter rapidly, giving it no second glance or afterthought. Then she rang, and bade her women send her the African boy Mahmoud. When he obeyed her summons, she gave him a letter.

'Take that to the château of S. Pharamond,' she said to him. 'You know Count Othmar. Wait until you can see him alone, and give it, when he is alone, into his own hands. You understand me.'

Mahmoud prostrated himself, put the letter in his vest, stretched himself again on the ground in obeisance, then silently left her presence.

She had always found the child obedient and intelligent, the only person in all her household who would obey implicitly and in silence, without feeling any curiosity as to the purport of his errands or ever babbling of them in the servants' hall.

When he had left her she remained long motionless, lost in thought, sitting alone amidst the dying roses, and the sunbeams broken and dimmed by the deep shadows from the veiled windows. She had a strange desolate sense of having given up the only thing which could have made life worth the living.

'But I think in what I wrote there was no suggestion of regret,' she mused, recalling all her written words. 'I think not; I hope not. If he believed that there were any regret on my side, it would be of no avail to have written it. He would be here in an hour, and he would follow me all the world over.'

Then she summoned her women again:

'I go back to Russia to-night to Zaraizoff,' she said to them. 'Tell Paul to have everything done that is necessary.'

CHAPTER LIV.

The boy Mahmoud, with the letter in his vest, took his way by the inland paths towards S. Pharamond; it was not more than three miles, following the tracks the peasants used. Mahmoud was almost always dumb, but he was ceaselessly watchful; he adored his mistress, but he was morbidly jealous of her. In the gay households of La Jacquemerille, of Zaraizoff, of the Hôtel Napraxine, his precocity had become familiar with all the corruptions of the world of white faces. Speaking little he was supposed to understand as little; but, in truth, the small listening dusky boy understood every word which went past him. He had heard them in Paris speak of Othmar; he had comprehended that Othmar was the lover of his mistress; he had heard Paul say to his friends, 'If it have ever been anyone, it is that one.' He had understood, and he had taken a hatred of Othmar into his silent, savage, volcanic child's heart.

When Mahmoud had been very ill with the cruel north winds which blew so bitterly on his lungs, made only to breathe the torrid air of the Soudan, his lady had come to see him, had spoken sweet words to him in his own tongue, had touched his dusky paw with her soft snowy hand. Mahmoud would have died a hundred deaths for her if he had had the chance; but he was jealous, like a little black sulking dachshund, of the mistress who sheltered him. Whenever he walked behind her, bearing her shawls or her sunshade, he could have kissed her shadow as it fell, but he could have plunged his dagger into the throats of the great gentlemen who sauntered by her side. He was furiously, blindly jealous, with the jealousy of a child and of a little wild beast blent in one. To his naturally evil passions the life of Paris had united a monkeyish malice and a precocious comprehension of vice. As he went now under the red blossoms of the pepper trees and the yellow flowers of the mimosas which fringed the route, a devilish fancy came into his head.

If, instead of giving the letter which he bore to Othmar, he took it to Othmar's wife? His faculties had been educated enough in all the scandals and jests of Paris to surmise that so he might bring about with impunity a complication not easy to unravel, a storm not easy to allay. If his mistake were ever brought against him, it would seem only a mistake; he would take refuge behind his stolid childish mask of affected stupidity, which had served him well more than once. He had the cunning of the African, and he knew that the first condition for his own safety in effecting such a treason would be that no one should observe him on his errand. He entered the grounds of the château cautiously. The gates usually stood open in the daytime, and the boy's gaily-clad figure glided in amongst the shrubs unperceived.

It was about five o'clock in the afternoon. Yseulte was seated out of doors, in a part of the gardens which was not in sight of the house. There was a large Judas tree there covered with its crimson blossoms; beneath it were some rustic chairs. She was reading, or affecting to read; the book was open on her lap. The crimson flowers every now and then, shaken by a south wind, fell down upon the unturned page.

Mahmoud had crept noiselessly about amongst the trees and plants, until he saw her, with that feline skill and silence which were natural to him, and had been developed by his life in the households of the Napraxines. He knew her well by sight; he had seen her constantly in Paris. He knew nothing of her otherwise, but he was French enough by education to be sure that for her to receive and read a letter addressed to her husband would bring about some dire disturbance.

So he approached her, bowing low as he had been taught to do, and tendered the letter to her.

'From Madame la Princesse Napraxine,' he said, repeating his salaam.

Yseulte took the letter with a strange tumult at her heart: she did not look at the superscription; she broke open the envelope with agitation and haste. It might be only a conventional sentence or two, an invitation or a farewell, or it might be some message of greater meaning. It seemed strange to her that Nadine Napraxine should address even the most formal words to her. She sat down under the boughs of the roseate Judas tree and read what was written, read it all with that instantaneous comprehension which comes to the brain in moments of intense excitement.

There were but a few sentences in all in it, but those had been written to Othmar, not to herself:

'I have read your letter. I believe all that is said in it. I doubt most things, but I have never doubted your love for me. If there be any consolation to you in knowing this, you may believe it to the full. I am certain that you would do all you say if I would accept the gift of your life. But I will not; for it is not yours to give, and I do not rob the innocent. My dear Othmar, I have seen your wife a few hours ago; I sought her, she did not seek me; and from my soul I pity her, though I am not too easily moved to pity. I pity her because she loves you so greatly, and yet in your life she counts for nothing. She would die for you, yet she will never be able to quicken a single beat of your pulse. The fault is not hers—you admitted that the last evening I spoke to you in Paris—but she only irritates when she would please you, she only wearies you when she should stimulate you. You will never care for her; she is a young angel, yet she will go unloved by you all her life. But if you cannot do more, you can spare her some pain, some dishonour; and I desire you to spare her that. Yours is the fault that she is now beside you; you were in haste and blind, and adventured a rash experiment; but it would be ungenerous in us both if we made her pay all the penalty of my indifference and your error. You have a strange madness for me because I am far removed from you; but I—who am not mad—I can see that honour says to you, and generosity says to me the same thing. I do not use the stale word duty, because neither you nor I believe much in it; but honour and generosity call upon us to protect a child who cannot protect herself, and perhaps even a little also to remember a dead man who cannot avenge himself. I do not speak to you as moralists would speak; I only mean that you must remember those obligations which, as they were taken up unasked, must be fulfilled out of sheer sense of common honour. You cannot force yourself to care for her, but you can force yourself to conceal from her that you do not. She is one of those women who easily and willingly believe. For myself, I would sooner hesitate to dishonour a dead man than a living one; so, I think, would you, if you only pause and think of it. If I listened to you now when I have repulsed you before, it would always seem to me as if I had not been brave enough whilst he was living, whilst he could have killed me or you, or done anything he chose. This is mere sentimental superstition, no doubt, but so it is with me. We will not meet again, not yet, at least. You will not be happy, of course, nor will you love your wife; neither happiness nor love is to be had at command. But you are just by nature; be just now; do not let all the weight of a mistake, which was wholly of your own seeking and making, lie upon a creature altogether innocent. She is not wise as we are wise, but she has a beautiful nature; she is purity itself; be grateful. I do not say forget me, for that you will not do; but live so that I may admire you and not esteem you a coward. We have both always lived for ourselves, let us endeavour for a change to live a little for others.'

The letter was signed in full 'Nadège Fedorowna Princess Napraxine.'

Yseulte had read it once unconsciously, all its words seeming to smite her brain together like the blows of many hands upon an unresting creature. She read it once again consciously, deliberately, word for word; then she rose and put it out towards the bearer of it.

'It is not mine,' she said, in a suffocated voice. 'Take it to Count Othmar.'

But the African boy had disappeared. There was no sound near her except the sound of the sea breaking on the marble steps of the landing stairs far down below.

'Take it, take it!' she said, mechanically holding the letter out to the empty air. Then she staggered a little; her eyes grew blind; she groped with her hand to feel for the trunk of the tree, and crept to it and sank down on the bench beneath it, insensible.

How long she remained there she never knew. Gardeners were near, trimming the banksia roses of a covered arcade, and below, on the edge of the sea, there were boatmen and fishermen, and not fifty mètres away, in the house, in his library, Othmar was sitting, awaiting the reply to his letter. But no one knew what had befallen her. After awhile she was awakened by the touch of a sea breeze which rising rustled in the boughs and fanned her face.

When she was aroused and raised herself from her stupor, she saw the note lying before her on the ground.

CHAPTER LV.

She remembered all that it had said. She saw as though it were written in letters of fire the fact that her husband would leave her for ever if another would stoop to accept the gift of his life. She saw the terrible, inexorable humiliation of the truth that she would only owe his fidelity, his presence, and his endurance of her in the future, to the forbearance of Nadine Napraxine.

There was no place left in her mind for reason or hope to hide in; it was all a blank desolation.

The pride, which was the strongest instinct in her, and the gratitude which was the strongest motive, were all that were left alive in the dull stupor which had overspread her brain. The one told her that every hour which Othmar spent beside her would be but as an alms cast to her by her rival; the other told her that her existence was the sole barrier between the man to whom she owed obedience, love, and fealty, and the joys which he coveted, the fate which he desired. Not alone was she herself as nothing in his life; but she was his gaoler, his burden of burdens, his one unchangeable regret and calamity. He had sought her out of mercy, generosity, kindliness; and now she was for ever in his path of life like a black shadow which hid the sunshine from his house.

She had known this, or most of this, for many months, but its cruel indignity, its dreadful truth, had never looked to her all that it looked now as she realised that pity for her unloved loneliness which made her rival relinquish her hold on her husband's life and refuse to accept the dishonoured allegiance which he offered. She saw in those few words, which had been written for Othmar's eyes alone, the finer impulses of generosity, the higher instincts of compassion, which had impelled Nadine Napraxine to remember her and to spare her when her husband had been willing to sacrifice her as the forest doe was sacrificed of old upon the altars of love. She did not blame him or hate him; she loved him always with the same loyalty, the same grateful, mute, and timid devotion. But all her life revolted in her at the thought that she would owe his enforced constancy to the intercession of the woman he adored; that she herself was nothing more, would for ever be nothing more, than as the clog of wood upon the captive's foot, keeping his steps for ever in one cheerless path. She did not reason; a stupor of horror had fallen upon her; she was only conscious of this one fact, that whilst she lived Othmar would suffer.

Inherent in her nature was the heroism of a race which had never feared death or danger, and the pride, sensitive as a nerve laid bare, which made pity intolerable, charity insult, life without self-respect unendurable. A delirium of shame was upon her. There was only alive in her one consciousness—that she would never consent to live to be a torture to him, never endure to be outstripped in generosity and in renunciation by the enemy of her life. She had loved him with all the tenderness and loyalty of her nature; she had done all she could to pay him back in gratitude and affection the immeasurable gifts she owed to him; but she had long known that she had failed, that she had no power to console or to beguile him. She was only a weariness to him, a chain upon his liberties, a companion undesired and irremovable, a thing useless and joyless, which, being lost, would be never missed and never regretted.

Nay, the gates of life closing for ever on herself would let the light of the future stream in, white and fair, across his path.

Her mind was dulled and her whole being strung to unnatural excitation; the many months in which she had shut her unuttered sorrow in silence in her own breast had in a manner disturbed the balance of her mind. That solitude in thought and absence of sustaining sympathy, which may be as bracing as the north wind to older or sterner lives, had to her youthfulness and timid susceptibility been fatal as the north wind is to the shyly-flowering spring. She had lost all hold on proportion in her lonely grief; she had become morbidly self-absorbed, and grew in her own sight a useless and undesired burden. All which remained distinct to her were her pride, which revolted from acceptation of her rival's intercession in her favour, and the piteous sense that no devotion, no sacrifice, no effort on her part could ever make her more in her husband's existence than a weight, a weariness, a thing undesired and unloved. The unselfishness and the loftiness of her instincts now served her worse than any fault or feebleness would have done. So long as she lived nothing, she knew, could serve him or release him. The patience and the piety which her confessor ceaselessly put before her as the eternal and unfailing panacea of woe could do nothing to give him happiness whilst she was there beside him; only her vacant place, her stiff dead limbs, her forgotten grave—these alone could be the precursors of any joy or liberty for him.

She did not reason thus, but she was moved by the knowledge of it, as one groping in the dark is guided by his touch. For the moment that sublime insanity of self-sacrifice was on her which has sent all the martyrs of the world to self-sought death.

By that which she believed divine law she knew that she was forbidden to loose the cord of life. To forestall the summons of God was to her implicit faith a guilt so dark that it would cast its shadow athwart all eternity. But as her people had flung themselves by choice upon the pikes of the revolutionists rather than outlive their king, so she was willing now to cast herself into the jaws of death rather than outlive the loss of hope, the loss of honour.

In her sight all his gifts, all his embraces, all the possessions with which he had dowered her, were but so much dishonour, being only the alms of pity and of charity, the forced atonement of a chill indifference. To live one other hour beneath his roof and by his side seemed to her, in all the dim, blind stupor of her thoughts, an indignity before which any death were blessed. She had the silent resolution and the endurance, meek yet dogged, of her Breton blood; these held her outwardly calm and restrained, while the delirium of self-sacrifice drove her headlong to her fate. She had never loved him more than she loved him at that moment. She had clearness of memory and strength of devotion enough to think, even in those terrible instants, of the only ways in which she could spare him pain. If he knew that her death was self-sought, remorse would be with him all his days.

'He shall not know; he shall not know,' she whispered to the sunny air and to the crimson blossoms.

She stooped and tore the letter of Nadine Napraxine into small pieces, and cast them down amongst the shrubs. Then with slow, unsteady steps she took the familiar paths which led through the gardens to the hills. There were no tears in her eyes; a flame-like force of self-destruction burned in her and scorched up all natural fear. Even the frightful guilt which her creed made her believe she was about to take upon her soul could not appal or arrest her. Even the human yearning in her which impelled her to turn back once and look upon his face and hear his voice,—if only from some distant place, as strangers might look and hear,—she had strength in her to resist and repel. Seeing him, she would betray herself; he would suspect; her death would be a burden to him as her life had been. She wished him to be happy, never to think of her save now and then with kindness.

Fortitude and self-denial were stronger in her than any other thing, and hushed down the natural revolt of aching passions.

'I will give him my life, since it is all I have to give,' she thought: she was his debtor for so much, but thus her debt would be paid.

She went slowly, but steadily, up the familiar way in the glad light of the afternoon hours. With the swift, unstudied instincts of a mind feverish and confused, but holding fast to one central and immovable idea, she had remembered at once the means by which she could reach her end and make her death seem the result of accident; she had remembered a crumbling tower on the flower-farm of her fostermother, where the owls built and the pigeons mated, and where again and again as a child she had been forbidden to risk life and limb on its rotten stairway and its ancient stones, but obstinately had sat for many an hour, seeming close to the blue sky, looking down on the olive and orange woods, and calling to the birds wheeling above her head.

One false step there—then silence. Who would ever know?

The sun was near its setting as she reached the hedge of aloes marking the boundary of S. Pharamond. She passed through them, and crossed a field or two where the red tulips were glowing beneath the tall wheat; then she reached the farm of Nicole Sandroz. No one was in sight: the man was away in the town of Villefranche, the women were at work in the rose fields. No one saw her save the old dog of the house, who gave her a mute welcome, creeping out with stiffened limbs from his niche in the wall. From the hill side on which the house stood, the turrets and terraces of Millo, the towers and woods of S. Pharamond, the green oasis of their gardens and the blue sea shining beyond, spread out before her gaze in all the glow and glory of the sunset hour. The golden light suffused all the visible world in its effulgence, and the mountains northward were violet as the cup of an anemone flower. She looked a moment: then closed her eyes and turned away, lest the fair sight of the earth at evening should weaken and unnerve her.

She entered the dwelling-place and ascended the stairway leading to the tower, relic of an ancient time when the low white-walled building had been fortified and armed against the pirates of the sea and the freelances of the land. She climbed the broken steps of stone, which her young feet had so often trodden with the careless light tread of the kid, and its heedlessness of danger. Every now and then a narrow slit in the masonry of the tower let in the golden light of the world without and let her see the smiling sunlit fields. A strong shudder shook her at such times from head to foot, but she did not pause until she had reached the platform of the tower. It was worn and broken, many fissures yawned in it, the unused nests of birds cumbered it, the battlements which had once protected it were almost levelled with its floor; the stones which remained were lose and uneven. She paused upon the summit, and the glory of the evening light was all about her and upon her; the deep blue heavens seemed very near. Though it was daylight still there were stars clear and large above her head. The world lay soundless and serene; no echo from it reached her through those depths of air.

Her eyes dwelt upon the place of her home.

The circling pigeons flew around her, the wind of their wings fanned her cheek. She kneeled down and made the sign of the cross.

'God receive my soul!' she murmured. 'It is guilt—but there is no other way.'

Then she rose, and, with a step which never paused or faltered, she walked to the edge of the undefended roof. She looked once more southward to where the house of Othmar lay, once upward to the vault of azure air.

Then she stepped forward into the void below, threw her arms outward as a bird spreads its wings, and fell, as a stone falls through the empty air.

A little while later the women coming there, called by the howling of the old house-dog, found her lying quite dead upon the turf beneath. Death had been merciful and had not mutilated her, her face was calm and had not been bruised or wounded: her head had struck upon a stone, and she had died without any lingering pain or conscious death-throe.

The birds were flying startled and distressed above the summit of the tower. The sun had set.

Her last wish was fulfilled.

No one dreamed that her death had been sought by her own will. The loosened masonry told its tale, and no one doubted what it said. She had accomplished that supreme sacrifice which is content to be unguessed, unpitied, and, attaining to the martyr's heroism, puts aside the martyr's crown.

L'ENVOI.

In a year from that time Nadine Napraxine sat in her white boudoir in her house in Paris.

It was the eve of her marriage with Othmar. She was lying indolently amongst her white cushions; her eyes were thoughtful, her mouth was smiling.

'If one could only feel all that rapture which he feels, how charming life would be!' she mused, with her old sceptical wonder at the ardour and the follies of men.

Passion was for once acceptable to her, but it was still scarcely shared; she still surveyed and analysed its forces with a vague astonishment, a lingering derision. Love had reached her more nearly and enveloped her more warmly than she had ever believed that it would do; yet there remained beneath it the smile of her habitual raillery, the doubt of her habitual incredulity. Her life had obtained the fruition of all its desires, and the future was hers in perfect triumph, so far as any human knowledge can possess it. Yet, in the vague melancholy which floated like a little cloud at times upon her careless and amused mockery of herself, she thought more than once of the device emblazoned on the wall of Amyôt, *Nutrio et extinguo*—it is the motto of all human passions.

'Yes, this is love, no doubt,' she said to him this day; 'it is even ecstasy—as yet. But shall we never know the recoil? Shall we never tire? Will there be no reaction, no fatigue, no level lengths of habit and of tedium? Who can keep always at this height?'

'We shall—for ever!' murmured her lover, with the intensity of his adoration for her trembling on his lips. 'To doubt it is to doubt me!'

'No,' said Nadine Napraxine, with her fleeting mysterious smile. 'No; I do not doubt you at all; I only doubt myself—and human nature!'

She sighed a little, even as she smiled. She, who had divined so much more of the truth than the blunter perceptions of a man had ever suspected, she, with that melancholy presage and superstitious sadness which were dormant in her blood, thought, with a passing chill of dread:

'Our joy is like the basil plant of Isabella. It blossoms out of death!'

THE END.

FOOTNOTES:

1. A fact.

Milton Keynes UK
Ingram Content Group UK Ltd.
UKHW030741071024
449371UK00006B/673

9 789362 092946